"'We face a brand new type of World War, one in which our opponent is ourselves—and our profligate burning of fossil fuels and the dangerous climate change it is causing. Like World Wars past, our only option is to mobilize and draw upon every tool at our disposal—in this case, to achieve no less than the decarbonization of the global economy. If you want to understand the challenge we face and what you yourself can do to help ensure a victorious outcome, read *Unprecedented Climate Mobilization: A Handbook for Citizens and Their Governments*."

—Dr. Michael Mann
Director, Earth System Science Center
Pennsylvania State University

"The climate emergency is unprecedented so we don't have well-proven protocols for handling it. We owe Woodworth and Griffin a debt of gratitude for being the first to step in with their Handbook to fill the gaping 'how to' gap. As the climate movement transforms itself to become the climate emergency movement, we will find the task much easier for being able to draw on this handbook."

—Philip Sutton
Co-author, "Climate Code Red"
Member, Climate Mobilization Advisory Board

"This powerful book by Woodworth and Griffin is an inspiring rallying cry, a call to action grounded in truth. The New Deal in the 1930s showed how, when the people demand action, both economy and society can be reshaped. But today we need to go further. The atmosphere on which we all depend is in grave danger, and we must address this danger as though our lives depended on it—because they do."

—Dr. Jill Stein
2016 presidential candidate for the
Green Party of the United States

"A very important book offering a detailed roadmap of the top-down climate mobilization, led by government, required to tackle climate change, together with a roadmap of the bottom-up mobilization by citizens using all available tools including social media. This essential handbook of what tackling climate change entails is required reading at a time when the principal existential threat to human civilization continues to be broadly ignored by governments, businesses and the financial markets."

—Assaad W. Razzouk
Clean energy entrepreneur
and commentator,
CEO of Sindicatum

"The Paris Accord acknowledges the need for global warming to stay 'well below 2 degrees Celsius' and to achieve 'net zero emissions' within a few decades. These goals have revolutionary implications. Committed to further expansion, accumulation, and consumption, the ruling corporate elite has offered no convincing leadership. Woodworth and Griffin's book lays out how — by embracing climate truth — movements, constituencies, and individuals can come together to create a new world from the ashes of the old."

—Sean Sweeney, PhD
Contributor to New Labor Forum
and coordinator of Trade Unions
for Energy Democracy

"Woodworth and Griffin argue persuasively that addressing the climate crisis requires societal transformation on a scale last seen during World War II. Such drastic changes in priorities will require enthusiastic participation from governments and all levels of society. The authors explain what concerned citizens need to do to make this happen."

—Andy Skuce
Contributor to *Skeptical Science*

"In a time of unprecedented crisis, it's time for an unprecedented popular movement to solve it. Against the incredible odds we face, Woodworth and Griffin outline what it would look like for people in key sectors of civil society to shift into 'emergency mode' and unleash the transformative power of climate truth by leading us toward the WWII-scale effort we need to secure our future. We have the tools — now it's up to us to mobilize."

—Margaret Klein Salamon, PhD
Founder and Director of
The Climate Mobilization

"The accelerating rate of global warming requires an urgent response that far exceeds the level of commitment shown by world leaders to date. The gap between climate change and climate action is widening. This book helps us to confront an unprecedented emergency that requires dramatic action – a World War II like mobilization."

—Rolly Montpellier
Editor for BoomerWarrior.Org

UNPRECEDENTED CLIMATE MOBILIZATION

A Handbook for Citizens and Their Governments

by

ELIZABETH WOODWORTH

DAVID RAY GRIFFIN

CLARITY PRESS, INC.

© 2016 Elizabeth Woodworth / David Ray Griffin
ISBN: 978-0-9972870-7-3
In-house editor: Diana G. Collier
Cover design; R. Jordan P. Santos

Participants at the 2015 United Nations Climate Change Conference photo by Antonio Fucito, used under the Creative Commons Attribution 3.0 Brazil license: http://agenciabrasil.ebc.com.br/en/internacional/foto/2015-11/presidenta-dilma-participa-da-cop-21

Peruvian Foreign Affairs Minister Reinel at the opening ceremony of the 2014 United Nations Climate Change Conference by Antonio Fucito, used under the Creative Commons Attribution-Share Alike 2.0 Generic license: https://www.flickr.com/photos/cancilleriadeperu/15312081713/

Climate Change Camp Protest at Heathrow Airport in London by Andrew, used under the Creative Commons Attribution-Share Alike 2.0 Generic license: https://www.flickr.com/photos/ nez/1181091743

Photo of David Ray Griffin by Haji Zainol Abidean, screen name Mahaguru58.

Clarity Press, Inc.
2625 Piedmont Rd. NE, Ste. 56
Atlanta, GA. 30324 , USA
http://www.claritypress.com

TABLE OF CONTENTS

FOREWORD

This latest climate crisis book by Elizabeth Woodworth and David Griffin is the most readable, most up-to-date blueprint for global survivability (which used to be sustainability). It is comfortably concise and elegantly and accurately written.

It will have great appeal to the growing climate mobilization movement, and the record two-thirds majority of Americans who now (in 2016) know that climate change is real and of real concern.

The evidence of the need for a global climate mobilization is overwhelming.

In just the few years since Griffin set to writing his long and comprehensive *Unprecedented: Can Civilization Survive the CO2 Crisis?*, published in February 2015, all the directly recorded effects of atmospheric greenhouse pollution have been accelerating faster than ever.

Climate mobilization is the imperative of all time.

Surface warming of the planet increased by a record amount in 2015, and 2016 is predicted to have another record increase. This is because atmospheric carbon dioxide (CO2) is accelerating at a record and unprecedented rate. Also, as a direct result of the atmospheric CO2 increase, ocean acidification is at a 20-million-year high and accelerating at an unprecedented rate.

Over 90% of the extra heat from greenhouse gas emissions has gone to ocean heating, which is destructive to ocean life. Subsurface ocean heating is accelerating. But much more potentially devastating is that heat to the deep ocean is accelerating even faster.

Ocean heating is killing off coral reefs below the ocean surface, causing deep-ocean dying zones from lack of sufficient oxygen.

Ocean heating, like global surface warming, is caused not only by CO_2 emissions but by the other two big global warming gases: methane and nitrous oxide. They are also at record highs and today are increasing extremely fast.

With the new – and obviously obscene – fossil fuel fracking industry, emissions from natural gas, which is mainly methane, are increasing. Greenhouse gas experts have established that the expansion of the natural gas industry is the cause of the increase in atmospheric methane.

The greenhouse emission, black carbon/soot, is now found to be second only to CO_2 in its warming contribution and therefore presents a huge opportunity for the climate mobilization to target.

The December 2015 United Nations Climate Conference in Paris was widely hailed as making great progress towards putting global emissions into decline. In retrospect, the Paris Agreement is little help and means more deadly delay, making climate mobilization absolutely essential.

The Paris Agreement did, however, recognize that the 1.5°C limit is safer than the old 2°C limit, which spells catastrophe (as Griffin argued in his 2015 book). For many years, the IPCC assessments have concluded that lower latitude (tropical / subtropical) populations would lose crop production at a small degree of warming. The 2014 IPCC Fifth Assessment Report (AR5) found that at 1.5°C, crop yields in the best food-producing regions in the temperate northern hemisphere would also suffer. We must all mobilize for food security everywhere.

The AR5 found that few land species can survive

a warming above 1.5°C, and that ocean acidification only stabilizes (at mid-century) under a 1.5°C scenario. We must mobilize to protect the natural world and oceans from the worst mass extinction of life ever.

We all need a global warming limit of 1.5°C, so we all need to mobilize – right now.

The IPCC 2007 4th Assessment Report stressed that global emissions must be on the decline by 2015. Global mobilization is imperative even for a 2.0°C limit and immediate mobilization is needed in order not to exceed 1.5°C.

But there is absolutely nothing in the Paris Agreement that will put global emissions on course for 1.5°C or even 2.0°C. The Paris Agreement relies only on voluntary, (non-binding) "intended" national emissions targets, called INDCs for "intended nationally determined contributions." Indeed, a recent report was titled, "The US isn't even close to its Paris climate agreement targets."[1]

Going in to the 2015 Paris Climate Conference, the UN Climate Secretariat calculated the combined emissions targets of world governments and found it would result in an increase in global emissions by 2030 – rather than the substantial decrease that the 2014 IPCC AR5 had called for. So it was expected that the 2015 Paris Agreement would put this right. But it didn't.

On 2 May 2016, the UN Climate Secretariat reviewed the latest post-Paris national emissions targets and found that they still lead to substantially higher global emissions in 2030. The Paris Agreement, as 350.org's Bill McKibben has said, means we have to work even harder to preserve our planet and our future. Going beyond the call for government mobilization, this book rightly calls for society to mobilize at every level.

The Paris Agreement did not include anything on the two measures we know will put fossil fuel emissions into rapid decline globally. These are: 1) terminating the trillions of dollars per year in fossil fuel subsidies worldwide (according to the International Monetary Fund), and 2) charging the fossil fuel industry the full costs of its planet-destroying and population-poisoning pollution – which would mean putting a price on carbon, a direct full carbon tax at source). The world must mobilize to force governments to stop pushing fossil fuels on the world and to stop destroying the planet for all future generations.

National leaders and candidates for leadership are blatantly obstructing any political progress in climate and ocean disruption mitigation. Progress in clean, renewable, zero-carbon energy is spectacular, but globally fossil fuel extraction continues to increase.

Something else outside of the international negotiations and beyond national politics is required, something right now, and something that acts fast.

That something is being recognized as emergency climate mobilization, though we know it is actually emergency mobilization for the climate system, which includes the oceans, the ice sheets and the great forests. This is the book for these times. Read it and pass it on and on for others to read and act on, as though our life depends on it – because it does, as David Griffin, Elizabeth Woodworth, and many others know.

Peter D. Carter, M.D.
Director, Climate Emergency Institute
Expert Reviewer, IPCC 5th Assessment, 2014

Endnotes

1 Katie Medlock, "Inhabitat," 6 October 2016.

PREFACE

We see little evidence that governments are coming to grips with global warming and the resulting climate disruption.

Much lip service is paid: global conferences continue, national reports are commissioned, bold words are spoken, the media report increasingly bad weather – but the sad reality is that governments continue to allow new oil drilling, pipeline construction, fracking operations, enormous military projects, the mass production of large consumer vehicles, and so on.

The summer of 2016 was the hottest since records began in 1880. The last time summer was this hot, human beings had not yet left Africa.

By October, the 12-month running-mean temperature had risen to +1.3°C relative to pre-industrial times, leaving little room in the 1.5°C budget. "Negative emissions" through reforestation and agricultural reform, said leading climate scientist James Hansen, are urgently needed to capture and store atmospheric carbon.[1]

We note a statement from the Center for American Progress in September of 2016:

> Here's a study that will ruin your afternoon: by the time today's kids are adults, there may be no more African elephants roaming the continent for which they are named. . . . Beyond elephants, we have bigger problems. In a world where carbon is priced too cheaply to reduce greenhouse gases, we're all doomed.

Government foot-dragging over carbon pricing is coming, as expected, from climate-change denial sponsored by the oil industry. But it is also coming from the fact not enough citizens and organizations have demanded it.

Little of consequence will bring carbon under control until citizens raise their collective voices so high that corporate donations and political lobbying will no longer dictate government policies.

We wrote this book with the hope that it will contribute to the movement – recently endorsed by the Democratic National Committee - to convince the American government to implement a World War II-type mobilization to save civilization from climate chaos.

Chapters 3-5 are based on the chapter "Mobilization" in Griffin's 2015 book, *Unprecedented: Can Civilization Survive the CO2 Crisis?* The remaining chapters were written primarily by Woodworth. But we both consider the work as a whole to be ours.

Elizabeth Woodworth,
Victoria, British Columbia
David Ray Griffin,
Santa Barbara, California

November, 2016

Endnotes

1   James Hansen, et al., "Young People's Burden: Requirement of Negative CO2 Emissions," Columbia University, October 4, 2016 (paper in review process)

ACKNOWLEDGMENTS

We wish to express our appreciation to all those who are trying, in large and small ways, to reduce the threat of global warming.

In particular, we are thankful to those whose work we have cited, and to those who have helped us with this book, including Dr. Sean Sweeney, for alerting us to President Franklin Roosevelt's Rural Electrification Administration; our indefatigable editor, Diana Collier; and especially Dr. Peter Carter, for contributing the foreword.

We also wish to acknowledge the ground-breaking work of the Climate Mobilization, founded by Dr. Margaret Klein Salamon. We are grateful to Philip Sutton of Melbourne, Australia, and co-author of Climate Code Red (2008), for his comments and perspectives.

Finally, we thank all of those who took time from their busy schedules to read and write blurbs for our book

INTRODUCTION

This little book is about problem solving for the climate crisis.

The nature and scope of the crisis has already been laid out in *Unprecedented: Can Civilization Survive the CO2 Crisis?* and will not be re-examined here.

Instead we will address the fact that in spite of decades of scientific warnings and UN engagement, governments have not stepped up to the plate.

The world desperately needs a deeply committed leadership and a program of action. The global public's growing presentiment of the horrific impact of global warming has enormous potential to shift society into "emergency mode."

Emergency mode can be much more readily aroused if a concrete solution is offered. It's a historical fact that once a threat has been squarely faced, entire nations have put normal living aside to shoulder massive efforts to overcome it.

However, there has been reluctance to use the word "emergency," which lies partly in the common experience that a crisis "emerges" suddenly. As in World Wars I and II, this grand scale climate disaster is "emerging" in slow motion – precisely because it *is* occurring on such a grand scale.

In this gradually developing context, pointing to America's WWII model as precedent, *Unprecedented Climate Mobilization* urges and informs a full WWII-style climate mobilization and leadership role for the United States.

It begins with how the American people have risen and adapted to "long emergencies," demonstrated in particular by President Franklin Delano Roosevelt's ability to mobilize Americans a full two years before the United States declared war on Japan, December 8, 1941, following the Pearl Harbor attack, and on Germany three days later.

US automakers had built three million cars in 1941. During the stepped-up mobilization that followed Pearl Harbor, they quickly converted their factories to making tanks and airplanes, producing only 139 passenger vehicles until the war ended in 1945.

Similarly, a sweeping conversion of America's outdated energy system to clean energy requires the political will to choose a survival response over our habitual lives.

The United States, China, and the rest of the world must now act with unreasonable haste, working together as if – to use Peter Goldmark's analogy – "some huge rocky projectile, big enough to destroy most forms of life, was hurtling towards the earth, and it seemed that deep international co-operation offered the only hope of deflecting the lethal object."[1]

As in the WWII effort, all sectors of society must be engaged – governments, the media, business, labor, religious groups, and the public at large.

Unprecedented Climate Mobilization offers every sector specific leadership possibilities, networking opportunities, and information resources to help.

It then surveys the tools of the lost arts of civil disobedience and nonviolent action that civil society will need — tools that won civil rights, brought an end to the Vietnam War, and served in the anti-nuclear campaigns.

Not least, the handbook shows how the democratically advancing social media can be applied in original ways to maximize personal influence. These social media tools are now so powerful that governments and news agencies continually monitor and analyze their Facebook posts and Twitter streams to gauge public opinion.

Although the December 2015 United Nations climate summit in Paris broke exciting new ground with a global agreement among all 195 countries to end the fossil fuel era, the agreed-upon schedule is a gradual one, and is not enforceable.

Another year has gone by, and gradualism isn't delivering the results that will save civilization.

Endnotes

1   Peter Goldmark, "Fiddling with Words as the World Melts," *Economist*, December 18, 2008.

Chapter One

THE TRANSFORMATIVE POWER OF CLIMATE TRUTH TO DRIVE AN "EMERGENCY LEVEL" RESPONSE

We all, as citizens of the planet, and regardless of our nationality, face the unprecedented existential threat of climate change.

We know that it is the top threat to the world's food supply, public health, and social security. We also know that eliminating fossil fuel emissions is our most urgent moral responsibility towards present and future life.

Actually declaring an emergency at a city or state or national level is a momentous kind of decision involving thousands or millions of people. Declaring war is an example, and it is not done lightly.

The truth about climate change, although a big enough threat to justify such a declaration, seems too distant and disturbing to invade our lives unless:

- we can envisage a collective mobilization plan that offers a good chance of success, and
- we can imagine transforming our lives in a positive way to engage in the plan.

Before turning to a mobilization plan in Chapters 3 and 4, we should look at the assumption that changing our lives to mount a general mobilization would be a painful disruption of our habitual activities in "normal mode."

What's in it for me?

"Emergency mode" is the zone that human beings enter when they are confronted by a sudden, dangerous crisis. Psychologist Dr. Margaret Klein Salamon, co-founder of the Climate Mobilization project, believes that climate activists should "use the transformative power of climate truth" to lead the public out of "normal mode" into "emergency mode," which is contagious.[1]

She begins by addressing the fear of some social theorists that mass panic and chaos will result if people are told the whole, graphic truth about unmitigated climate change.

This defeatist view of the human spirit has been adanced by authors in the literature of psychology and sociology, which has helped keep the truth suppressed. The supporters of this view overlook the amazing grit and resourcefulness that ordinary people so often display during major, life-threatening emergencies.

Dr. Peter Carter is a Canadian physician, climate activist, and expert reviewer of the 2014 IPCC 5th climate change assessment. He believes that dealing with emergencies is what has characterized human survival for aeons, which is precisely why we exist as a species today.

Indeed, a published mental health study reports benefits associated with responding to climate change:

The challenges of climate change "may galvanize creative ideas and actions in ways that transform and strengthen the resilience and creativity of community and individuals... Seligman's work on positive psychology, with its focus on the relation between mental health, hope, and optimism, provides strong support for the potential for growth and transformation to emerge from the climate crisis.[2]

Such transformation might induce public action on climate change mitigation and adaptation: "vivid focusing events, changes in public values and attitudes, structural changes in institutions and organizations capable of encouraging and fostering action, and creation of practical and available solutions to the problems requiring change."[3] Dr. Salamon writes of emergency mode: "This mode of human functioning, markedly different from "normal" functioning – is characterized by *an extreme focus of attention and resources on working productively to solve the emergency.*"[4]

This extreme focus has been described as an intense type of "flow state." Flow is "an optimal state of consciousness when we feel our best and perform our best." It's the same as "being in the zone," which athletes sometimes experience.

People in the zone speak of time slowing down so much that the moment to act gives them ample time to complete it. Tennis players speak of the ball moving so slowly that they can return it with ease and perfection. Accidents are often reported as occurring in slow motion. In short, the "zone" is an altered state of the nervous system that is a key part of our natural survival equipment.

Mihaly Csikszentmihalyi, the psychologist who pioneered the "flow" concept, described it as:

Being completely involved in an activity for its own sake. The ego falls away. Time flies. Every action, movement, and thought follows inevitably from the previous one...your whole being is involved, and you're using your skills to the utmost.

So there is a discrepancy between the emergency we imagine as a brief and scary interruption of life-under-control, and the actual experience of living through it.

In short emergencies, such as fires, people may enter and remain in the flow state until the emergency ends.

Long Emergencies

In "long emergencies," the business of normal life is built into an extended emergency response, and the flow state alternates with rest, recreation, and relationships.

Long emergencies exist all around us: fighting chronic illness, cancer, and debilitating accidents; struggling through poverty to meet basic needs; fleeing from fire; and coping with war.

Many professionals – doctors, nurses, paramedics, crisis counselors, firefighters, police officers, and soldiers – integrate emergency mode day by day.

A variation of "long emergency mode" is "long *moral* emergency mode," when situations such as *apartheid* that undermine dignity and liberty become so acute that normal life pales before the great struggle for justice.

The decision to enter long moral emergency mode is based on the clarity and immediacy with which an existential threat is perceived. During *apartheid*, for example, people were immersed in the moral struggle for justice for over 40 years.

The looming crisis of climate change is both a long moral and a long existential emergency. While cultural immersion in the emergency has been stunted by its virtual absence in political and media discourse, it has not – incredibly – been a question the media has put to US presidential candidates during election debates.

But things are changing. Since 2014, the enormous climate marches have shown that we are approaching the flow state we need to be in, in order to enter emergency mode on a broad grassroots scale.

In July, 2016, a motion by Russell Greene to declare a WWII-style climate emergency was passed almost unanimously at a full Democratic Party Platform Committee meeting. It noted:

> Democrats believe it would be a grave mistake for the United States to wait for another nation to lead the world in combating the global climate emergency. In fact, we must move first in launching a green industrial revolution, because that is the key to getting others to follow; and because it is in our own national interest to do so. Just as America's greatest generation led the effort to defeat the Axis Powers during World War II, so must our generation now lead a World War II-type national mobilization to save civilization from catastrophic consequences. We must think beyond Paris. In the first 100 days of the next administration, the President will convene a summit of the world's best engineers, climate scientists, climate experts, policy experts, activists and indigenous communities to chart a

course toward the healthy future we all want for our families and communities.[4]

There was great excitement when this motion passed.

Armed with the transformative power of climate truth, Russell Greene had entered emergency mode in such a compelling way that he transferred its energy to the Committee.

Dr. Salamon believes that the best strategy for climate activists is to go into emergency mode themselves.

We need to get in the flow, communicate with others about the climate crisis and the need for emergency mobilization, and make it clear that many of us are already in emergency mode.

We all need to be in that mode. Once there, we will find how contagious it is.

The Need for a Clear Path to Effective Action

Unified action is inconceivable without a common goal and a plan that will unite everyone for the public good.

So far, governments have undertaken sporadic, isolated programs – rather like putting fingers in the dyke – but no coordinated all-out mobilization, commensurate with the enormity of the problem, has yet emerged.

In the next chapters we will examine the basics of such a plan.

Endnotes

1   Margaret Klein Salamon, "Leading the Public into Emergency Mode: A New Strategy for the Climate Movement," 2016, 2-3.

2   Fritze, J. G., et al., "Hope, despair and transformation:

Climate change and the promotion of mental health and wellbeing," International Journal of Mental Health Systems," 2(13), 2008, p. 9.

3   "Psychology and Global Climate Change: Addressing a Multi-faceted Phenomenon and Set of Challenges," American Psychological Association," 2009, p. 48.

4   Salamon, "Leading the Public into Emergency Mode," 4.

5   "Climate Mobilization Added to Democratic Party Platform," July 11, 2016 (https://www.youtube.com/watch?v=UwVJQ7rj3Go).

Chapter Two

WWII "EMERGENCY MODE" AS CLIMATE MOBILIZATION MODEL

1. What is Mobilization?

The idea of mobilization first appeared during the organization of troops and supplies for war in mid-nineteenth-century Russia. In the twentieth century, massive national mobilizations were mounted during World Wars I and II.

Mobilization entails a "long emergency" on a grand scale. It is triggered by a national threat (such as war) requiring the reorganization and re-directing of resources from the domestic economy to the war effort. As such, it must be led by the state, which must engage the cooperation of all citizens and all sectors of society.

Mobilization also implies that time is of the essence. The idea that a nation can win a war by gradually mounting a leisurely defense is fantasy. Similarly, climate change is progressing quickly and requires immediate and decisive action against our own habits and behavior. The idea that we can turn carbon emissions around gradually (or incrementally) without changing our lives – or how the various sectors of society (business, education, media, military, religion, government echelons) conduct themselves – is delusional.

Climate is at the heart of earth's weather systems and is the very foundation of our lives. Earth, as life's platform for existence, contains all things necessary for life. We must not take in stride the increasing (and alarming) rates in the rise of global temperatures, atmospheric CO_2, and ocean acidification.

If we pursue "gradualism," it will play out as an array of random, disarticulated efforts amounting to a vast, blind, ill-chosen negligence. We must call a halt to this approach, where governments and stakeholders wrangle over unenforceable agreements and resolutions to phase in distant measures that will not upset their special interests, or our habits and general comfort.

What does serious and responsible mobilization look like?

II. Features of the U.S. Mobilization during WWII

Background:

Following WWI, the Great Depression of the 1930s brought severe economic hardship to a defeated Germany. This created fertile ground for radical politics and brought to the fore Hitler's vision of a strong nationalistic Germany based on military expansion.

From 1935 to 1939, the Nazis developed combat munitions far exceeding those of any other country. By contrast, in 1939 the United States Army ranked 39th in the world.

Germany began its march through Europe by occupying Czechoslovakia's Sudentenland in October, 1938, and invaded Poland a year later on September 1, 1939. Britain, France, Canada, Australia, and New Zealand declared war on Germany within days, but Germany had already gained an enormous head start over these countries and continued ravaging Europe and Britain.

In December, 1941, the United States finally entered the war after the Japanese strike on Pearl Harbor. The extent of U.S. mobilization is stunning:

> The U.S. government was willing to spend as much money as needed to win the war. The federal budget increased from $8.9 billion in 1939 to over $95 billion in 1945. The gross national product, which is the total value of all goods and services produced by the nation's economy, increased from just over $90 billion to almost $212 billion. The total amount of war materials produced by 1945 was staggering. U.S. factories had made 296,000 warplanes, 86,000 tanks, 64,000 landing ships, six thousand navy vessels, millions of guns, billions of bullets, and hundreds of thousands of trucks and jeeps. U.S. production alone had exceeded the combined production of the Axis powers.[1]

Such a uniquely effective mobilization model could be applied to the more fundamental threat of global warming. Its features – some surprisingly beneficial – are outlined below.

1. President Roosevelt Declares National Emergency and Mobilizes for WWII

America was slow to formally declare war, but she did declare a national emergency more than two years before entering WWII.

In 1939, after ten years of the Depression, the American public was in no mood for another war abroad. A powerful isolationist movement had kept the general public and the business world in denial about the gathering storm in Europe.

American factories were in full peace-time consumer production, using oil, rubber, and steel to build more than three million cars a year.

Nonetheless, when war broke out in Europe in early September, 1939, President Roosevelt began taking emergency action. It's important to note that these emergency presidential powers were legally exercised for two years and two months, despite the fact that during that time the nation was not at war – and indeed was oriented against it.

Roosevelt first proclaimed "a limited national emergency" on September 8, 1939, and began strengthening national defense "within the limits of peacetime authorizations."[2]

On the same day, Roosevelt also issued an Executive Order stating that within the Executive Office of the President, there will be "in the event of a national emergency, *or threat of a national emergency*, such office for emergency management as the President shall determine." [our italics][3]

The Office for Emergency Management (OEM) was formally established within the President's Office eight months later – still pre-war – by his presidential Administrative Order of May 25, 1940.[4]

On January 7, 1941 (still 11 months before the U.S. declared war), President Roosevelt issued an Executive Order pursuant to his September 8, 1939, Executive Order 8248 that had accompanied his proclamation of "limited national emergency".

This order further defined the Office of Emergency Management, and outlined the functions of the new Office of Production Management to be created within the OEM.[5]

The government had recognized that the stakes were too high to permit the war economy to grow in an uncoordinated, laissez-faire manner.

The function of the Office of Production Management was "to increase production for the national defense through mobilization of material resources and the industrial facilities of the Nation."[6]

On May 27, 1941, in recognition of Hitler's worldwide objective to "dominate peoples and economies" and to overthrow the democratic world order, Roosevelt issued a formal proclamation of an *unlimited* national emergency, calling upon the nation's material and moral powers:

> I call upon all loyal citizens to place the nation's needs first in mind and in action to the end that we may mobilize and have ready for instant defensive use all of the physical powers, all of the moral strength and all of the material resources of this nation.[7]

By the time Pearl Harbor was attacked on December 7, 1941, billions of American dollars had already been diverted to re-arming.

Soon after Pearl Harbor, President Roosevelt told Congress and the country:

> It is not enough to turn out just a few more planes, a few more tanks, a few more guns, a few more ships than can be turned out by our enemies. We must out-produce

them overwhelmingly, so that there can be no question of our ability to provide a crushing superiority of equipment in any theatre of the world war.[8]

Roosevelt then set stunning goals for American factories: 60,000 aircraft in 1942 rising to 125,000 in 1943, and 120,000 tanks and 55,000 anti-aircraft guns in the same time period. To coordinate the war agencies, he created the War Production Board in 1942 and the Office of War Mobilization in 1943.[9]

Whereas business leaders had been bitterly opposed to Roosevelt's New Deal during the Depression, they now fully cooperated by joining government and labor leaders to tackle these ambitious targets.

With all sectors of the economy working together, U.S. military expenditures rose from $4.5 billion in 1941 to an incredible $20 billion during 1942. Germany fell behind in the space of one year, spending only $8.5 billion.[10]

The WWII-mobilization model above is an indication of the extent of mobilization that is now required and is indeed possible.

In considering WWII as a parallel to the "long" climate emergency today, we must emphasize that just as emergency presidential powers were used for more than two years before the United States joined the war effort, so too, today's long emergency of climate change warrants a replication of Roosevelt's precedent-setting use of presidential powers. This would be greatly assisted by a nationwide citizens' demand for a governmental climate mobilization, which would override (if not win over) any conceivable Congressional opposition.

Extraordinary Conversion of the U.S. Automobile Factories

As noted above, in 1941, more than three million cars had been manufactured in the United States.

In February, 1942, the government banned private automobile production and only 139 more cars were made during the war.

According to Lester Brown, auto companies represented "the largest concentration of industrial power in the world."[11] They were soon turning out three quarters of the nation's aircraft engines, half the tanks, and a third of the machine guns.

Chrysler made tanks and fuselages. General Motors made airplane engines, submarine engines, guns, trucks, and tanks. Packard made Rolls-Royce engines for the British Air Force. Ford produced jeeps, armored cars, troop carriers, gliders, and amazingly produced one B-24 Liberator long-range bomber every 63 minutes.[12]

Although auto-makers had resisted government controls at first, their vital contribution to the war effort was rewarded by an increase in their profits and production capacity for the future.

2. Funding the WWII Mobilization Without Causing Inflation

The government was the only customer for armaments coming off the assembly lines and the only employer of the troops. The total cost of the U.S. war effort was $296 billion (1945) dollars, the equivalent of more than four trillion dollars today.[13]

To fund this crisis, the U.S. government raised taxes by lowering personal exemptions, and by progressively taxing high incomes. A tax on excess corporate profits provided 25% of revenues during the war.

The government also moved into large-scale deficit spending (spending more than incoming taxes).

Rationing was imposed on commodities, rubber, and metals needed for the war effort. The "Victory Speed" limit was posted at 35 mph and driving for pleasure was banned. Ration books were issued by volunteers to civilians, limiting a wide range of food consumption from sugar and coffee to meat, cheese, butter, and canned goods.

But these strategies alone could not finance a war of such magnitude. *War Bonds* with long-term interest were issued annually and highly advertized – not only in the United States, but in Canada and Britain – inviting the whole country to invest. People flocked to buy them, a quarter being purchased by individuals and the rest by corporations and financial institutions.[14]

These funding strategies, designed to keep inflation under control, involved every member of society in a fair and united effort to conquer a long emergency.

3. Mobilization of all Citizens and Sectors of Society

In addition to rationing, everyday life across the country was dramatically altered for civilians. Millions of students, retirees, housewives, and unemployed moved into the active labor force.

To help build the armaments necessary to win the war, women were employed as electricians, welders and riveters in defense plants and shipyards while men were serving overseas. Women also worked on farms, and as streetcar conductors. They volunteered for the Red Cross and provided recreation to men in canteens.

Individuals and communities conducted drives

for the collection of scrap metal, aluminum cans and rubber, all of which were recycled and used to produce armaments.

To supplement rationing, Americans grew their own food in "victory gardens." By 1945, some 20 million such gardens were in use and accounted for about 40 percent of all vegetables consumed in the U.S.

4. Home Front Equality Was Essential to the War Effort

Administering the war effort on the home front required transparency that made people feel equal in their sacrifices.

Rationing was preferred to cumbersome taxes on limited goods. It was considered the best way to cut consumption quickly and to ensure that scarce resources, such as gasoline, tires, butter, coffee, meat, and cheese, were shared out equitably.

The steep "Victory Tax" on high incomes reached 94% in 1944. The most progressive tax in American history, it worked to equalize disposable income.

Full employment meant improved access to jobs and enhanced social equality for women, Latinos, and African Americans, who were still living under apartheid in the South.

5. Full Employment and an Economic Boom

Unemployment ended with the mobilization for war. Out of a labor force of 54 million, unemployment fell in half from 7.7 million in spring 1940 to 3.4 million in fall 1941, and fell in half again to 1.5 million in fall 1942, and to an all-time low of 700,000 in fall 1944.[15]

Employers were required to accept unions and to maintain their memberships. Organized labor expanded from 10.5 million members in 1941 to 14.75 million in 1945, a record high.[16] This boom flowed over into the peace economy.

Conclusion

Solving the "long emergency" of WWII had required a *reorientation* of:

- government's normal priorities
- society's normal resource allocations, and
- individuals' gratification and self-esteem activities, by spurring them to "do their part" to engage with the emergency.

This redirection of production and life-purpose away from consumerism towards an overriding national purpose bonded people in spirit, promoted egalitarianism, and greatly stimulated the economy as a whole.

It is important to remember that this transition from consumer production to war production was both demanded and supported by the federal government – whose leadership and coordination role was indispensable to its success. Although corporations played a vital role in mobilization, it was government that planned and implemented the survival strategy.

The initial steps in government leadership may already be in the cards with the Democratic National Convention's motion to adopt a WWII-type national mobilization in July, 2016, and the US national Green Party sharing the same position.

Endnotes

1   "World War II Mobilization, 1939-1943" (http://www.

encyclopedia.com/article-1G2-3424800081/world-war-ii-mobilization.html).

2 "Proclaiming a Limited National Emergency. Proclamation No. 2352, September 8, 1939 (http://quod.lib.umich.edu/p/ppotpus/4926579.1939.001/22). The wording of this proclamation is referred to in the much later PROCLAMATION OF UNLIMITED NATIONAL EMERGENCY, May 27, 1941 (http://www.ibiblio.org/pha/policy/1941/410527a.html).

3 "Executive Order 8248. Reorganizing the Executive Office of the President," September 8, 1939 (http://www.presidency.ucsb.edu/ws/?pid=15808).

4 This Administrative Order is cited in Executive Order 8629, January 7 1941 (http://www.presidency.ucsb.edu/ws/?pid=16114),

5 "Executive Order 8629 on the Office of Production Management and the Office for Emergency Management," .January 7 1941 (http://www.presidency.ucsb.edu/ws/?pid=16114).

6 Ibid.

7 PROCLAMATION OF UNLIMITED NATIONAL EMERGENCY, May 27, 1941 (http://www.ibiblio.org/pha/policy/1941/410527a.html).

8 Ken Burns and Lynn Novick, "The War: War Production," WETA, Washington, DC, 2007 (https://www.pbs.org/thewar/at_home_war_production.htm).

9 Ibid.

10 Mark Harrison, "Resource mobilization for World War II: the U.S.A., U.K., U.S.S.R., and Germany, 1938-1945," *Economic History Review*, 41:2 (1988), pp. 171-192 (https://www2.warwick.ac.uk/fac/soc/economics/staff/mharrison/public/ehr88postprint.pdf).

11 Lester R. Brown, "Plan B: Rescuing a Planet Under Stress and a Civilization in Trouble. Chapter 11. Plan B: Rising to the Challenge: A Wartime Mobilization," Earth Policy Institute, 2003 (http://www.earth-policy.org/books/pb/pbch11_ss3).

12 Ken Burns and Lynn Novick, "The War: War Production," WETA, Washington, DC, 2007 (https://www.pbs.org/thewar/at_home_war_production.htm), and Doris Kearns Goodwin,

"No Ordinary Time: Franklin & Eleanor Roosevelt: The Home Front in World War II," Simon & Schuster, 1994, 362.

13   Stephen Daggett, "Costs of Major U.S. Wars," Congressional Research Service, June 29, 2010, 2 (https://www.fas.org/sgp/crs/natsec/RS22926.pdf).

14   Ken Burns and Lynn Novick, "The War: War Production," WETA, Washington, DC, 2007 (https://www.pbs.org/thewar/at_home_war_production.htm).

15   Wikipedia, "United States home front during World War II," June 27, 2016 (https://en.wikipedia.org/wiki/United_States_home_front_during_World_War_II).

16   Blum, John Morton, "V Was for Victory: Politics and American Culture during World War II," New York: Harcourt Brace, 1976, 140.

Chapter Three

US PRESIDENTIAL LEADERSHIP AND IMPLEMENTATION OF CLIMATE MOBILIZATION

Authors' Note: This section is based on the hope that President-Elect Donald Trump will come to take science, especially the science of global warming, seriously. If he does not, then this book's proposal for mobilization would depend even more heavily on other agencies and social sectors. Congressional Democrats and also Republicans, who increasingly accept the science, could also provide leadership.

A Gallup poll taken March 2-6, 2016, found that 41% of US adults feel global warming will pose a "serious threat" to them during their lifetimes, and 64% said that they are worried about it.[1] The public is already attuned.

However, the governing and corporate sectors continue to respond in an incremental, piecemeal way, which is not going to reduce emissions fast enough to lower atmospheric CO_2 to 350 ppm.

There is a fundamental disconnect between the scale of the emergency and the scale of our response to it. We need a centrally-coordinated emergency mobilization to convert the economy from fossil fuels to clean energy.

Such a mobilization can only be mounted by the US federal government.

Historic Calls for an Emergency Mobilization

Over the past ten years, leading figures have called for a WWII-type mobilization for the climate:

- In his 2007 book *Hell and High Water: The Global Warming Solution*, physicist Joe Romm proposed that: "This national (and global) re-industrialization effort would be on the scale of what we did during World War II, except it would last far longer."[2]
- In 2008, James Hansen, the world's best-known climate scientist, wrote: "The most difficult task, phase-out over the next 20-25 years of coal use that does not capture CO2, is Herculean, yet feasible when compared with the efforts that went into World War II. The stakes, for all life on the planet, surpass those of any previous crisis."[3]
- In 2009, Lester Brown, described by the *Washington Post* as "one of the world's most influential thinkers," published a book entitled *Plan B 4.0: Mobilizing to Save Civilization*, in which he said that this effort "will take a massive mobilization – at wartime speed."[4]
- In 2010, journalist Ross Gelbspan said that we "need to mobilize like the WW II mobilization, but worldwide and even more thorough."[5]
- In 2011, Lester Brown reiterated: "The mobilization must be unprecedented, because the entire world has never before been so threatened."[6]
- Also in 2011, executive directors of the Sierra Club, Greenpeace, 350.org, and other organizations signed an Open Letter to Presidents Barack Obama and Hu Jintao, calling for the United States and China to reduce emissions by

80% (based on 2006 levels) by 2020 through a "wartime-like mobilization."[7]

- In 2012, Joe Romm said: "If humanity gets truly serious about emissions reduction – and by serious I mean "World War II serious" in both scale and urgency – we could go to near-zero global emissions in, say, 2 decades and then quickly go carbon negative."[8]

- From 2014 to the present, many US elected officials and political candidates have signed the *Pledge to Mobilize*,[9] including this partial list of such candidates running in the 2016 election: Dr. Margaret Flowers, for US Senate, Maryland; attorney Darren Soto, currently Florida State Senator, running for Congress; Wendy Reed, running for Congress, California; attorney Rob Hogg of the Iowa State Senate; and Green Party candidate for Congress from New York, Matt Funiciello.

- In April 2016, presidential candidate Senator Bernie Sanders, speaking on MSNBC, said that in WWII "the United States had to fight a war on two fronts in a very short period of time. And within three years, actually we had essentially won the war. I look at climate change almost in military terms… [W]e are being attacked and the attack is coming from climate change."[10]

- In July 2016, The Democratic National Convention added this statement to the 2016 Democratic Platform: "We believe the United States must lead in forging a robust global solution to the climate crisis. We are committed to a national mobilization, and to leading a global effort to mobilize nations to address this threat on a scale not seen since World War II."[11]

- During 2016, U.S. Green Party candidate Jill Stein's election platform included the statement: "Initiate a WWII-scale national mobilization to halt climate change, the greatest threat to humanity in our history."[12]

These calls for emergency mobilization are now more urgent than ever. As of May 19, 2016, business-as-usual carbon emissions would allow only 5 years before the world blows past the 1.5°C carbon budget.[13]

Presidential Authority to Declare a National Emergency

Does the threat to earth's climate constitute the required threat level to satisfy the legal requirement for declaring a national emergency? Various characterizations of a national emergency would indicate that it does. For example:

- Declaring a national emergency, said famous professor of constitutional law Edward S. Corwin, "connotes the existence of conditions suddenly intensifying the degree of existing danger to life or well-being beyond that which is accepted as normal."[14]
- Declaring that a climate emergency exists, professor of environmental policy John J. Berger wrote: "An emergency has two basic components: it presents a grave threat to life, liberty, property, or the environment, and the situation requires immediate action."[15]

The idea that we are in just such a planetary emergency is acknowledged by many:

- In 2006, Al Gore published his book *An Inconvenient Truth,* with its subtitle: *The Planetary Emergency of Global Warming and What We Can Do About It.*
- In 2007, UN Secretary General Ban Ki-moon said climate change "is an emergency and for emergency situations we need emergency action."[16]
- In 2012, John Bellamy Foster and Brett Clarke wrote an article for the *Monthly Review* entitled "The Planetary Emergency."[17]
- "The truth is," said James Hansen in 2012, "we have a planetary emergency."[18]
- In 2013, *The Nation* published "The Coming 'Instant Planetary Emergency'" by Dahr Jamail, who noted that because of climate change, scientists predict that the future of the planet "will be nothing short of a nightmare."[19]

As we saw in the WWII precedent in Chapter 2, the individual most important to declaring a national emergency is the president of the United States. There are many things that the president could do, similar to what Roosevelt did in 1941.

Most important, the president could proclaim a *national climate emergency* and issue an Administrative Order to create an Office of Emergency Climate Management within the Office of the President. An American president cannot, of course, declare a planetary emergency, but can, as stated above, give an Administrative Order to create an Office of Emergency Climate Management for the United States.

The same Order could also create an Office of Clean Energy Production Management within the President's Office, to plan and coordinate the vast scaling up of various types of clean energy, such as solar, wind, tidal, and geothermal.

According to the *National Emergencies Act* of 1976, the president would need to specify what statutory authority or stand-by laws would be activated by the declarations. In this regard, there are "470 provisions of federal law delegating to the executive extraordinary authority in time of national emergency."[20]

For example, the president might use the US Environmental Protection Agency (EPA), which regulates greenhouse gasses under the *Clean Air Act*.

Certainly having Congress onside would be a great advantage. But if not, the president could issue the declarations and invite citizens to urge their members of Congress to support them. (Non-violent citizen strategies are listed in Chapter 6.)

Presidential Announcement of Targets and Incentives

While issuing the emergency proclamation, the president could identify the targets and incentives most needed to lead the conversion and build cooperation:

- A clear commitment to below 1.5C long term target (equlibrium warming)
- A clear commitment to below 350 ppm CO_2, and below 400 ppm CO_2 equivalent
- A goal of zero-net-emissions[21] from energy, transportation, and agricultural systems to end the fossil fuel era by 2030
- An 8% annual decrease in carbon emissions, to be ordered immediately
- Placing a stable, predictable tax on carbon, and using it to subsidize clean energy businesses,

including green buildings and electric autos and trains

- Provision of subsidies assisting eligible fossil-fuel companies to convert to green energy, if conversions were performed at 8% of operations per year
- The creation of venture-capital programs for the clean-tech sector
- Placing carbon import taxes on all products for which a carbon tax was not paid in the country of origin
- Including a global carbon tax in the UNFCCC negotiations
- Charging corporations the full costs of pollution (e.g. livestock meat industry, nitrogen chemical fertilizers, steel and cement buildings[22])
- Banning halocarbon and sulfa hexafloride GHGs nationally and globally
- Controlling black carbon soot through the EPA air quality powers, as it is second only to CO_2 in warming contribution
- The US and all govts should right now be implementing the IPCC AR5 best case scenario RCP 2.6.[23]
- Proposing rationalization of the fixed-to-fail extraordinary voting procedure for the UN negotiations[24]
- Mandating the use of only known reserves of gas and oil until 2030; halting exploration for new reserves immediately
- Leaving dirtiest fossil fuels, including coal, tar sands, and shale oil, in the ground starting no later than 2025, and no later than 2018 for tar and shale
- Moving the U.S. Government toward a WWII-

style economy where required to mobilize against climate change, raising the capital to fund massive infrastructure conversion projects to be completed by 2030:

- Office of Emergency Climate Management to coordinate the installation of the various types of clean energy, to make the grid entirely green by 2030
- Radically upgrading the electric grid to facilitate the distribution of clean energy
- While the grid is greening, phasing in electric vehicles – including motorcycles, autos, SUVs, vans, and trucks
- Phasing in high-speed rail for passengers and freight by 2030, replacing airplanes as efficiency dictates
- Subsidizing the development of fossil-fuel-free airplanes
- Rationing oil and gas for automobiles and home heating
- Subsidizing electric vehicles, home heat pumps, rail and ship travel, and urban public transport and bicycling

Implementation Powers of the President

The presidency brings with it a number of tools to lead this conversion:

Executive Powers: The president could ask Congress for executive powers to expedite the U.S. response to the emergency, similar to FDR's War Production Board and his Controlled Material Plan. If Congress refuses, the president could use the *Clean Air Act*, as noted above.

Executive Agreements: It has become customary for presidents to work out binding agreements with leaders of other countries without the need for Congressional consent. Such agreements are now more common than treaties. The president could work out reciprocal agreements to reach zero net global emissions by 2030.

Powers as Commander-in-Chief of the Armed Forces: In this role, the president could declare that the major security threat to the country is climate change, rather than other countries or terrorists. Consequently:

- A much larger part of the Defense Department budget could be allocated to climate security
- More of the DoD budget could be used to increase energy efficiency within the military and to provide technologies for the general economy
- DARPA (the Defense Advance Research Projects Agency) could be tasked with speeding up the development of new energy technologies
- The military could share its efficiency and clean energy expertise with other countries, consolidating friendships by uniting against global warming

Special Sessions with Congress: In special sessions, whether open or closed, the president could explain to Congress the need for the new policies, and respond to objections. These sessions, plus meetings with relevant committees from both Houses, should be held before votes on new policies, stressing that the fossil fuel lobby must no longer be allowed to influence voting in view of what is at stake and the extent of public demand for significant action.

Bully Pulpit: The conspicuous position of the president gives him the "bully pulpit" (named during

Teddy Roosevelt's presidency) to inform, educate, and lobby on behalf of the need for an all-out mobilization to save civilization. The president needs to consolidate the enthusiastic support of the American people and thereby assure the full cooperation of Congress.

Fireside Chats: Part of the "bully pulpit" could be frank talks by the president similar to FDR's "fireside chats," explaining the proposed climate policies, quelling false rumors, and offering encouragement. Presidents may also use weekly radio addresses, and may arrange with cable networks for weekly, televised discussions with the public.

Climate Corps: Using the bully pulpit, the president could invite a "climate corps," mobilizing millions of citizen volunteers. The Climate Corps could:

- lobby to get the president's agenda through Congress
- target resistant members of Congress at election time, explaining to voters why it is important to replace them
- arrange for teach-ins around the country, led by educators, scientists, economists, engineers, doctors, and others, as done during the Vietnam war
- modeled on the Peace Corp, send capable people to other countries to assist with energy efficiency programs, and to learn from them as well

Convening Power: To promote understanding and agreements, the president can bring various parties together, such as:

- Governors and the mayors of major cities in various regions of the country, to discuss how they can work together.

- The owners and program directors of the major television networks, radio stations, and newspapers, explaining how vital their role is to the climate emergency response (see Chapter 4 on the media).

The Federal Role in Building the New Energy Economy

There are many economic parallels between today's energy conversion emergency and the WWII arms production emergency. Both cases require(d) rapid industrial transformation.

The relevance of the WWII economic model is shown below.

Massive Government Spending for WWII Arms Production: The federal government poured billions into the war effort. It employed more than 10 million Americans through the vastly expanded military.

It also signed large war production contracts, financed by deficit spending, progressive taxation, and War Bonds, causing the greatest industrial building boom in history. At the peak of the war effort in 1944, defense spending constituted 41% of GNP, up from 2-3% in 1939. After the long Depression, unemployment was quickly wiped out, dropping from 14.6% to 1.9% in five years. Some 17 million jobs were created, wages grew 55%, and corporate profits soared.[25] Most importantly, the war against fascism was won.

Similarly, an all-out federal investment in conversion to a clean energy infrastructure could work to solve many problems at once:

- *Massive Government Spending in the Transition to Clean Energy:* Most commercial corporations have failed so far to respond to the climate threat in a meaningful way. Only the federal government, with its ability to make large-scale investments in R&D, public infrastructure, labor, and assembly line production, can plan, motivate, implement and enforce the transition at the necessary scale and urgency.

- *Rapid Expansion of Green Industries*: Net-zero carbon industries, which serve a small fraction of current energy demand, could be quickly built up through contracts and subsidies.

- *Production Control of Fossil Fuels*: A ban on all new fossil fuel mining and power generation infrastructure could act to limit fossil fuel supply and send a strong market signal that the fossil fuel era is over. The government could also order the early retirement of fossil-fueled power plants and their related infrastructure.

- *Economic Tools:* Money creation, deficit spending, progressive taxation, climate bonds, and price controls could be used to rapidly increase demand for zero-carbon energy technologies, reduce demand for fossil fuels, contain inflation, and fairly distribute resources during the mobilization. The *Climate Bonds Initiative* is an international green-bond not-for-profit "focused on mobilizing the $100 trillion bond market for climate change solutions."[26]

- *Rationing*: A rationing system could also be used to sharply cut emissions and channel scarce resources to the national net-zero carbon infrastructure. WWII showed that the government must convince the public that the rationing system is transparent and equitable, and that evaders are few and likely to be detected and given stiff penalties if found guilty.

- *Carbon Tax:* Raising the tax on carbon could be offset with a reduction in income taxes, thereby shifting investments from fossil fuels to renewables.

- *Expanding the role of the military:* To help the American economy to transition out of its dependence on military spending, the military could be re-assigned from costly and unpopular missions abroad to build the national electricity grid with transmission lines; an electric vehicle charging network; wind, solar, and geothermal installations; municipal public transport; and solar shipping and aviation.

- *Civilian Job Creation:* The government's role in a vast job creation initiative could be to use public funds as incentives to leverage far greater investments of private capital.[27]

- *Research & Development:* Much research is required to develop methods to remove greenhouse gases from the atmosphere, improved renewable energy power storage, and agricultural techniques that reduce the carbon footprint. The federal government could assign contracts to innovative businesses, university researchers, and technical colleges to lead high-tech climate advances.

- *International cooperation:* In WWII, the U.S. allied with many nations in a massive, cooperative effort to defeat fascism. During the climate mobilization, the U.S. could engage the rest of the world, including large nations such as China, India, and Russia, in an urgent, cooperative transition to a sustainable, post-carbon civilization.

The US could supply other nations with aid and technology, and in turn could borrow from their successes.

One such success is the German *Energiewende*,[28] or "energy transition," to create a low carbon, environmentally sound, reliable, and affordable energy supply. The new system relies heavily on wind, photovoltaics, and biomass; also on energy efficiency and energy demand management. Most existing coal-fired generation will be retired, and the phase-out of Germany's nuclear reactors is scheduled for completion in 2022.

Participatory Planning and Shared Sacrifices

Roosevelt's government used a "participatory planning" approach in areas such as housing, by creating national goals that left many planning decisions to local communities and individuals.

A climate emergency administration could engage people in the same way, enlisting their skills and contributions while restoring a safe climate.

Properly managed, the actions outlined above could successfully curb climate change – as long as the media get caught up in it.

Endnotes

1   Oliver Milman, "A tipping point': record number of Americans see global warming as threat," *The Guardian*, March 18, 2016.

2   Joseph Romm, *Hell and High Water: The Global Warming Solution* (New York: Harper, 2007), 235.

3   James Hansen et al., "Target Atmospheric CO_2: Where Should Humanity Aim?" *Open Atmospheric Science Journal* 2 (2008), 217-31.

4   Lester Brown, *Plan B 4.0: Mobilizing to Save Civilization,* W.W. & Norton Company, 2009.

5   Ross Gelbspan, "Rewiring the World with Clean Energy,"

The Heat Is On (website), 2010.

6   Lester Brown, *The World on Edge: How to Prevent Environmental and Economic Collapse* (Norton, 2011), 96.

7   "Open Letter to President Barack Obama and President Hu Jintao," 19 January 2001.

8   Joe Romm, "The Ghost of Climate Yet to Come," *Climate Progress*, 25 December 2012

9   "Public Servants Who Have Pledged to Mobilize," The Climate Mobilization (http://mobilized-leaders-tcm.webflow.io/).

10   "Bernie Sanders: We Must Move on Climate as We Would if We Were at War," Climate Emergency Declaration, 13 May 2016. For video, see "Bernie Sanders Talks Climate – and WWII-Scale Mobilization" (https://www.youtube.com/watch?v=4hSwVUZC5Eo).

11   Joe Romm, "Democratic Platform Calls For WWII-Scale Mobilization To Solve Climate Crisis," Climate Progress, 22 July 2016; see "2016 Democratic Party Platform July 21, 2016."

12   Jill Stein, 2016 Platform (http://www.jill2016.com/platform).

13   CarbonBrief, "Analysis: Only five years left before 1.5 °C carbon budget is blown," May 19, 2016 (http://www.carbonbrief.org/analysis-only-five-years-left-before-one-point-five-c-budget-is-blown).

14   Edward Samuel Corwin, *The President, Office and Powers: History and Analysis of Practice and Opinion* (New York University Press, 1941). Corwin's definition was quoted in Harold C. Relyea, "National Emergency Powers," Congressional Research Service report for Congress, Updated August 30, 2007, p. CRS-4 (https://www.fas.org/sgp/crs/natsec/98-505.pdf). Discussion of the stand-by laws and provisions is found on p. CRS-3.

15   John J. Berger, "In 2013, a Climate Emergency Exists," *Sante Fe New Mexican*, 1 July 2013.

16   Juan Lose Lagorio, "UN's Ban Says Global Warming Is 'An Emergency,'" Common Dreams, 11 November 2007.

17   John Bellamy Foster and Brett Clarke, *Monthly Review* (December 2012), 1-25.

18   "We Have a Planetary Emergency: Hansen, Leading NASA Climate Scientist, Urges Unions to Act," Cornell Universi-

ty, 23 October 2012.

19   Dahr Jamail, "The Coming 'Instant Planetary Emergency,'" *The Nation,* 17 December 2013.

20   Relyea, "National Emergency Powers."

21   We define "net zero emissions as "zero emissions of carbon dioxide and other long-lived greenhouse gases such as methane and nitrous oxide." The International Panel on Climate Change (IPCC AR5) is right to say "near zero" because even 100% changing our energy production (to zero carbon), our agriculture and our diet, it is not possible for us to not emit any of the 3 GHGs.

22   Using engineered wood products instead of concrete would sink carbon for hundreds of years.

23   This is our very last chance to stabilize surface temperature and ocean acidification, without resorting to planet geoengineering - which will not work in any case (https://static. secure.website/wscfus/8154141/3861276/rcp-26-temp-emissions-text-aug-16.png).

24   The UNFCCC requires decision by consensus. This has been wrongly interpreted as virtual unanimity or a 100% vote, as in the 2016 Paris summit.

25   Margaret Klein Salamon, "The Case for Climate Mobilization," [2015], 8.

26   This remarkable organization has an Advisory Panel from 21 countries and helps to certify green bonds to a high standard.

27   Lester Brown estimated that $100 billion of federal funds used strategically over 12 years would leverage $400 billion of private capital investment. If this $500 billion were allocated evenly between renewable energy development (wind, solar, and geothermal) and retrofitting, and if every two jobs created in the energy sector created one job elsewhere, this would quickly generate 600,000 new jobs that would last through 2030. Lester R. Brown, "Plan B Updates: Creating New Jobs, Cutting Carbon Emissions, and Reducing Oil Imports by Investing in Renewable Energy and Energy Efficiency," December 11, 2008 (http://www. earth-policy.org/plan_b_updates/2008/update80).

28   "Energy Transition: The German *Energiewende*" (http:// energytransition.de/).

Chapter Four

MEDIA LEADERSHIP IS ESSENTIAL

History of Wartime Media Leadership

During WWII, war correspondents accompanied the troops on planes, ships, and on the front lines. Their first-hand news and radio broadcasts brought the war's vivid struggle into family living-rooms and to their movie theater newsreels.

The government regulated this news, which had to go through the Office of War Information (OWI). Sixteen hundred members of the press were accredited by the armed forces to report on the war in such a way as to keep domestic optimism alive. War casualties were not allowed to be shown.

As the years wore on, public complacency set in, so the government began to show graphic images of death and destruction on the front lines. This increased the sales of War Bonds.

The United States and other WWII nations papered their cities with posters and billboards to keep the public engaged in a justifiable war response. (This can be done more easily today with TV and radio.)

Regrettably, since then, while Cold War and terrorism *propaganda* has evolved with technology, reporters and journalists have gained little more independence from their agencies than during WWII.

The Corporate Media Today

With only five US television networks remaining, the media enjoys an unprecedented concentration of power, whereby it manipulates public opinion.[1] The "news" is often in lockstep with corporate interests, especially during election years.

To successfully mount a climate mobilization – a mobilization against a deeper, more enduring public threat – the president would again require the full cooperation and leadership of a corporate media that grasps the existential nature of the emergency, one which will not spare them, either.

Massive government-generated or -sponsored advertising campaigns and news coverage of climate-caused events and documentaries could replace and compensate for any losses due to withdrawal of advertising related to fossil fuel use.

Such cooperation can only be ensured by highly visible, insistent demands by civil society to be kept fully informed of the climate dangers that motivate "the climate effort," and of developments related to that effort itself. Indeed, the agreement reached by all 195 countries at the Paris climate summit in December 2015,[2] was driven by enormous climate marches in cities around the world that neither the press nor national governments could ignore.

Media Betrayal of the Public Trust

The corporate media conglomerates should be pressured to take renewed stock of journalism's ethical roots and responsibilities to democracy and the common good.

In 1988, Edward Herman and Noam Chomsky wrote that the mainstream media exists to manufacture public consent for the powerful elite.

Exemplifying this were the "935 lies" told by seven of the top Bush administration officials, which were used to promote the 2003 US-led invasion of Iraq.[3]

Critical journalists and analysts raised serious questions about these White House lies at the time, but their warnings were mostly ignored by corporate media networks.

In fact, top media personalities were dismissed for doubting the claims that Saddam Hussein had weapons of mass destruction. Phil Donahue, in spite of his high ratings, was fired from MSNBC for presenting "a difficult public face in a time of war," while MSNBC's competitors were "waving the flag".[4]

BBC journalist Andrew Gilligan, its chairman, Gavyn Davies, and director-general Greg Dyke, resigned under fire for claiming that the British government had "sexed up" a report claiming that Saddam Hussein had WMDs.

These journalists were right to object. The Iraq war, which cost millions of lives and untold misery and is still fracturing the peace and stability of the Middle East and Europe, was condemned by the British Chilcot Inquiry in July, 2016.

In March, 2015, the international Ethical Journalism Network (EJN), a global coalition of 50 journalism and media support groups, reported that the rot goes further down:

- media managers are making deals with advertisers to carry paid-for material disguised as news

- editors are being bribed by politicians and corporate managers

This corruption is making it increasingly difficult to separate journalism from political propaganda and from corporate PR.

The EJN report exposed the external pressures that journalists increasingly face worldwide, noting the similarities experienced by many countries.[5]

With regard to climate change, an April 25, 2016 study by *Media Matters* showed that in the weeks following announcements that 2015 was the hottest year on record, and that February 2016 was the hottest month on record, CNN aired five times more fossil fuel ads than climate reports. Only one of CNN's three reports about temperature records mentioned climate change or global warming. In addition, the combined climate coverage on ABC, CBS, NBC, and Fox decreased 5% from 2014 to 2015, despite landmark actions to address global warming.[6]

As the global climate tips dangerously toward chaos, it is essential that honest media professionals at all levels challenge the political and corporate agendas. One way would be to emphasize, wherever possible (e.g., on individual Twitter pages, where employees often qualify their opinions as personal, not corporate), the time-honored ethics of journalism that are publicly stated by news outlets.[7]

In summary, the climate emergency requires that the news be driven less by profit than by social responsibility to the planet and its future inhabitants.

Restoring the Public Standing of the Media

The idea of the public trust goes back to the origins of democratic government. Its essence is that the true power and future of a society rests with the public, and that whatever trust the public places in its officials must be respected.

The fourth estate has long been entrusted with central control of society's communications and therefore has a unique fiduciary responsibility to the public good.

In their book, *"The Elements of Journalism: What Newspeople Should Know and the Public Should Expect,"* Bill Kovach and Tom Rosenstiel write that the first purpose of journalism is

> to provide people with the information they need to be free and self-governing ... Its first obligation is to the truth ... its first loyalty is to citizens.[8]

Most professional journalists and editors understand and respect this, but they obviously do not own the media, whose ethics bend under influence.

Kovach and Rosenstiel cite Peter C. Goldmark, Chairman and CEO of the *International Herald Tribune,* saying that corporate media leadership has a "solemn fiduciary responsibility arising from their ownership of a news organization – that they hold a public trust."[9]

With respect to climate change, this public trust held by corporate owners lies at the heart of civilization's survival. They must be brought to view the problem as real and needing their help.

Kovach and Rosenstiel say that the news *must be comprehensive and proportional to the significance of events,*[10] and that

> the purpose of news is to help people self-govern, but that only begins with giving people the information they need to do so. News must also be about solving the problems that confront individuals and the community.[11]

The authors also explain that people need the news to act for them as their "empowerer":

> Providing audiences with tools and information so they can act for themselves. This involves making information interactive, providing dates when action needs to be taken, explaining how to get more involved. It may go even further and involve organizing events that bring the community together to solve problems.[12]

The foregoing argues for the overriding duty of the corporate media to assume a leading role in addressing the climate disaster.

Chapter 7 will provide social media strategies to make the media do just this.

What the Corporate Media Should Stop Doing

The media should be made to recognize that it has been guilty of supporting the fossil fuel companies by promoting a false climate debate – at the risk of destroying civilization. It must be made to understand that it should no longer:

- Suggest that climate scientists are divided on the reality and cause of climate change
- Frame reports by climate scientists in "both sides" news coverage, giving equal time and credence to the views of denialists
- Publish editorials expressing skepticism about climate science

- Cite "dark money" sources, such as the Franklin Center's *Watchdog*, financed heavily by the Koch Brothers through Donor's Trust[13]
- Ignore or tone down scientific reports for the sake of not alienating advertisers
- Accept false claims in climate advertisements from fossil-fuel corporations
- Exclude climate change from television's Sunday morning talk shows, which continued to focus more on climate denial in 2015,[14] thereby implying that it is not very important
- Reduce climate change coverage in evening news broadcasts from ABC, CBS, FOX, and NBC and MSNBC, which dropped to an overall total of 73 minutes in 2015.[15]
- Ignore the connection to climate change while reporting extreme weather events.

Things the Media Could Do to Foster Climate Mobilization

Instead, the media could reform itself, by doing everything it can to lead the country in coping with the climate emergency by:

- treating the climate threat to civilization as the overwhelmingly most important story of our time – just as U.S. newspapers and films did all they could to mobilize America to address the threat of the Axis Powers
- reporting on the climate effort aimed at mitigating rising emissions as seriously and extensively as it treats extreme weather
- criticizing networks and newspapers that support climate denial, explaining why their behavior is

not just irresponsible but reprehensible

- limit advertizing   that encourages fossil fuel consumption, or carry equal free advertising time for clean energy
- adopting socially engaged journalism in the spirit of Danny Schechter, who reported what was happening, why it was happening, and why other media outlets did not tell the whole story[16]
- informing the electorate about which candidates for various offices are especially good and especially bad with regard to climate legislation
- consulting media content analysts such as *Fairness & Accuracy in Reporting* (FAIR.org), which document media bias and censorship, and *Project Censored: The News that Didn't Make the News,* and as a result
- legitimately promoting themselves as a home of straight talk when it comes to climate

Beyond correcting the defects in their previous treatments of the climate threat, the media could, in the spirit of Kovach and Rosenstiel, develop programs to educate people about climate change and inspire them to do what they can. For example, there could be:

- High-quality series (such as Showtime's "Years of Living Dangerously"[17]) subsidized and made freely accessible to the entire viewing public
- Talk shows with informed hosts interviewing the world's leading climate scientists, along with politicians, economists, and others grappling with climate change, promoting presidential action, and explaining, among other things, how the president's policies can move the nation towards a solution

- A series, perhaps entitled "Climate Denial Exposé," that explains how climate denialism has been orchestrated by the Koch brothers and the fossil-fuel companies; how they fund front groups, so the denials appear to come from ordinary people; and how much money they have funneled to members of Congress who support denialism
- Similarly, a series perhaps entitled "Climate Offenders," to educate the public regarding which companies and stocks to avoid
- An ongoing entertainment show featuring comedians lampooning climate denialists
- Along with stock market daily updates, the updating of climate developments, including atmospheric CO_2 readings, and the remaining gigatons in the global carbon budget

Corporate media owners must be made to understand that the choice they make – whether to continue supporting fossil fuels, or to help citizens and their governments rise to meet the climate crisis –will have a profound impact on the future of civilization.

Endnotes

1   According to Noam Chomsky, "propaganda is to democracy as the bludgeon is to a totalitarian state," and the mass media are the primary vehicle for delivering propaganda in the United States. Noam Chomsky, "Media Control: The Spectacular Achievements of Propaganda," Seven Stories Press, 2002.

2   Although COP21 has been (rightfully) criticized for not going far enough, it did manage to gain the signatures of all 195 nations on an agreement to hold the world to a 1.5 C rise in temperature. The best that was expected was 2 C.

3   Charles Lewis, "935 Lies: The Future of Truth and the De-

cline of America's Moral Integrity," Public Affairs, Washington, D.C., 2014; Appendix B.

4   "Phil Donahue on His 2003 Firing from MSNBC, When Liberal Network Couldn't Tolerate Antiwar Voices," March 21, 2013 (http://www.democracynow.org/2013/3/21/phil_donahue_on_his_2003_firing). An internal NBC report surfaced to explain the cancellation of Donahue's show: FAIR: Fairness & Accuracy in Reporting, "Iraq and the Media: A Critical Timeline," March 19, 2007 (http://fair.org/take-action/media-advisories/iraq-and-the-media/).

5   "Corruption in the media is killing ethical journalism, says EJN," March 16, 2015 http://europeanjournalists.org/blog/2015/03/16/corruption-in-the-media-is-killing-ethical-journalism-says-ejn/).

6   Kevin Kalhoeffer, "STUDY: CNN Viewers See Far More Fossil Fuel Advertising Than Climate Change Reporting: Following Temperature Record Announcements, Oil Industry Ads Outpaced Climate-Related Coverage By Almost 5-To-1," April 25, 2016 (https://mediamatters.org/research/2016/04/25/study-cnn-viewers-see-far-more-fossil-fuel-advertising-climate-change-reporting/209985). CNN ranks #1 in prime time cable news.

7   ASNE. American Society of News Editors. "Ethics" (http://asne.org/content.asp?contentid=236). See also, "ASNE Statement of Principles" (http://asne.org/content.asp?contentid=171).

8   Bill Kovach and Tom Rosenstiel, "The Elements of Journalism: What Newspeople Should Know and the Public Should Expect," 3rd ed., Three Rivers Press, 2014, 9.

9   Ibid., chapter 1.

10   Ibid., 9.

11   Ibid., 29.

12   Ibid., 28.

13   Joe Strupp, "Franklin Center Top Donor Is Right-Wing's 'Dark Money ATM,'" Media Matters for America, February 22, 2013.

14   Media Matters for America, "How Broadcast Networks Covered Climate Change In 2015" (https://www.scribd.com/doc/302896750/Media-Matters-Climate-Broadcast-Study).

15   Ibid.

16   John Nichols, "Danny Schechter Was Our News Dissector," *The Nation*, March 20, 2015.

17   YEARS of Living Dangerously (http://yearsoflivingdangerously.com/).

Chapter Five

LEADERSHIP
IN OTHER SECTORS

If the United States is to take its share of responsibility for the climate crisis – and to provide the kind of leadership that it should be providing – all sectors of America must be mobilized. For mobilization to succeed, members of every profession and skill must pitch in.

Academic Leadership

College, university, and graduate-school professors have excellent leadership opportunities. In addition to writing books and articles, giving lecture tours, creating new courses and centers (such as Vanderbilt's Climate Change Research Network), they may provide:

- *Community leadership:* For example, David Orr, Professor of Environmental Studies and Politics at Oberlin College, has led a joint venture between the college and the town to create a thriving, sustainable community, which designed the first green building on a U.S. campus.
- *Political statements:* For example, Ethics philosopher Professor Lawrence Torcello of

the Rochester Institute of Technology teaches climate justice. He has argued in a blog post that those behind well-funded efforts to deny global warming should be criminally prosecuted.

- *Divestment encouragement:* In 2016, Daniel Kammen, Distinguished Professor of Energy at UC Berkeley, wrote a "Statement on Fossil Fuel Divestment for the American Association of University Professors," urging Governing Boards to divest endowments and retirement funds from fossil-fuel holdings.
- *Educational non-profits*: The Alliance for Climate Education intends to reach 20 million high-school students by 2020 with its program training students to become climate leaders.

Activist Leadership

To get the country seriously mobilized, activists – including those who use civil protest and disobedience – need to lead by example. Here are a few cases of people providing leadership:

- Bill McKibben, the world's best-known green journalist, founded the first climate-change grassroots movement, 350.org. It has organized, for example, climate marches and high-profile global divestment campaigns.
- Earth sciences professor James Hansen has taken action in various ways, from testifying to Congress about climate change in 1988, to being arrested multiple times for civil disobedience, to reaching out to young people through his blog and supporting their efforts.
- Al Gore's *Climate Reality Project* has nearly 50

staff and 7 branch managers. Its mission is "to catalyze a global solution to the climate crisis by making urgent action a necessity across every level of society," and to create a critical mass of activists to transform the politics of the climate crisis.

- A new organization named *Climate Mobilization* urges and defines a WWII-style approach to a complete clean energy conversion by 2030.

NOTE: Hundreds of climate activist organizations are listed in the Open Directory of the Internet (DMOZ).[1]

Agricultural and Forestry Leadership

Agriculture uses 70% of the world's water and emits vast quantities of methane and nitrous oxide. US agribusiness is mono-cultural, energy-intensive, and heavily dependent on chemical fertilizers and pesticides. It could reinvent itself in various ways. For example:

- Wes Jackson's *Land Institute* has been advocating evolutionary biology, in which annual grain crops, which degrade the soil, are replaced by perennial grains, which preserve complex natural ecosystems.
- If Organic Regenerative Agriculture becomes widely used, it will do much to reverse global warming.[2]
- Center for Food Safety's Cool Foods Campaign shows how to take CO_2 out of the air and plug it into the soil, thereby reducing both global warming and ocean acidification.[3]
- No-tillage farming produces bigger crops as well as conserving the soil, as exemplified by No-Till on the Plains.[4]

- Fetzer Vineyards has become a leader in economically and ecologically sustainable organic wine-making. Besides employing efficient and clean energy, the winery builds the soil, sequesters carbon, and conserves biodiversity. Its Bonterra vineyard is the largest seller of organic wines in the country – mainly because its wines, compared with organic wines of yesteryears, are amazingly good.

Warmer forests are facing a perfect storm of threats from diseases and invasive pests. Reforestation worldwide could extract about 100 gigatons of carbon from the atmosphere. Deforestation must be stopped. Leadership is shown by:

- The *Plant a Billion Tree* projects, which are run by the Nature Conservancy, create healthy forests in the U.S., Brazil, and China by planting seedlings and through natural regeneration to help the forest heal.
- The science-based *American Forests* non-profit, which advocates the protection and expansion of U.S. forests, has planted more than 45 million trees since 1990, thus restoring watersheds and preserving water.
- The Pinchot Institute has reported that more than half America's forests are privately owned, mostly by people over 65. To sustain these carbon-capturing family forests intergenerationally, owners may profit by applying for carbon credits.

Business Leadership

Corporate Knights, a Toronto-based investment advisory

firm, compiles the annual Global 100 Index, which ranks the leading world corporations on best practices for energy productivity, carbon productivity, and ten other sustainability indicators. BMW heads the list. In 2015, the U.S. was first with 19 companies, and France was second with 11.

Yvon Chouinard, the founder of Patagonia — called by *Fortune* the "coolest company on the planet" – wrote, together with Vincent Stanley, a best-selling book entitled *The Responsible Company: What We've Learned from Patagonia's First 40 Years,* in which they explain how they learned to make the company progressively more responsible.

A growing number of businesses are working towards being 100 percent green. For example:

- Tesla Motors leads the world in electric vehicles and battery storage. Tesla has entered the mass car market and sells cars in China and Australia. It has installed a network of high-powered Superchargers across North America, Europe and Asia, and is building an immense Gigafactory in Nevada to bring down battery costs.
- Apple reported that in 2015, 100% of its energy use in 23 countries came from renewable sources, including all its data centers.
- Google is buying electricity directly from wind farms near its data centers, and by 2016 had invested nearly $2.5 billion in solar and wind projects.
- IKEA, which produces more than a third of its own energy using solar and wind power, has committed to be 100% green by 2020. It began selling solar panels in its retail stores in 2016.

Congressional Leadership

If the Congress is deadlocked over climate change, individual members should not give up, letting all of their informed passion go to waste. Instead, they should appeal directly to the public, explaining why the country needs to mobilize as fully as possible.

Action has already been taken by individual senators. For example:

- Hawaiian Brian Schatz organized 30 Senators in an all-night speech-athon that was covered by *The Guardian.*
- Senate leader Harry Reid called attention in July of 2016 to "the web of denial financed by the Koch Brothers and other fossil fuel interests."
- Senators Barbara Boxer and Bernie Sanders wrote a climate bill that included a carbon tax.
- Boxer and Sheldon Whitehouse created a Climate Action Task Force.

Leadership in Divestment

The fossil fuel divestment movement challenges institutions, individuals and governments to show climate leadership by divesting from their investments in fossil fuels.

Using the hashtag #keepitintheground, leaders such as *The Guardian*, 350.org, Pope Francis, the World Council of Churches, the Green Party, and the Carbon Tracker Initiative (which coined the term "carbon bubble") have inspired massive divestment.

Cities, states, universities, and pension fund managers now announce divestment decisions almost daily. By February 2016, over 500 organizations with $3.4

trillion in assets had committed to divest, with the Bill and Melinda Gates Foundation divesting in 2016.

Leadership by Economists

Recent economic studies have shown that mitigation (prevention) of global warming is far less expensive than adapting later to extreme weather events.

Many media writers and lawmakers evidently do not know this. Economists in the United States should do as Britain's Nicholas Stern has done, using TV, radio interviews, and op-ed pages to shape and focus the discourse on climate change, for which he won a Frontiers of Knowledge award.

Economists in academia, government and business need to flood the media with articles and op-eds showing that economists commonly advocate a steep price on carbon as the best deterrent to fossil fuel use, along with eliminating fossil-fuel subsidies.

Elders Leadership

Elders, as people with free time, are well positioned to provide climate leadership.

- *Elders Climate Action* believes that the responsibility to raise climate change awareness falls especially to elders, who throughout history have had a long view and commitment to future generations.

  Its Congressional Climate Project works "to create relationships of respect and appreciation with all members of Congress," not expressing preferences for candidates, but simply urging all to commit to action on climate change.

- *Conscious Elders Network* invites elders to join their "multi-ethnic, multi-faith, intergenerational, interdependent society founded on respect for the inherent rights of all living beings on a healthy planet, with an equal opportunity economy and a peace centered culture." The Network holds marches for a clean energy revolution.

Entertainment Leadership

A 2010 article, "Charismatic Megafauna," described celebrities as "intimate strangers" who bring climate change "into our living rooms and lived environments." The authors argue that a "multiplicity of climate change media and media forms is as crucial to getting climate change 'work' done as the climate science itself."

The media and their viewers, listeners, and readers are concerned with what celebrities have to say about the environment. Climate ambassadors such as Leonardo DiCaprio, Harrison Ford, Robert Redford, and Paris Hilton have great influence in countering the false claims of climate contrarians.[5] These figures influence cultural politics by connecting the formal science to everyday Western culture. Local entertainers in cities and towns have a parallel opportunity.

Dramatic films can be used to portray the specter of climate reality and to illustrate people doing their share and taking leadership.

Financial Leadership

Wall Street bankers and brokers are the primary conduit through which oil industry investments are raised from the public. Brokers encourage widespread investments, for example, to support fracking. In keeping with the extent to which it is invested in fossil fuels, Wall Street has generally appeared hostile to attempts to regulate emissions. Money from green-oriented billionaires is needed to counteract the enormous sums spent by the Kochs and fossil-fuel companies for climate denialist activities.

Former hedge fund founder Tom Steyer was influenced by Bill Gates and Warren Buffett to pledge much of his money to charity, and by Bill McKibben to take political climate action. Steyer founded NextGen Climate to support U.S. candidates, elected officials, and policymakers who will take bold action on climate change.

Steyer and fellow billionaire Michael Bloomberg, along with Goldman Sachs banker-turned-activist Henry Paulson, assessed in their report, "Risky Business" the economic risk exposure that specific industries have to global warming.[6] The study urged the financial community to reject the anti-scientific claims of Murdoch's media and the Kochs, and to transform the culture of the financial sector.

Nearly 150 billionaires have made the Gates-Buffett "Giving Pledge"[7] to commit half their money to charity, and in July, 2016 had raised $365 billion to, as one man said, "help build a more peaceful, equitable, and sustainable world." These and other billionaires could help to finance a full climate mobilization.

Governments and banks have started to raise money to mitigate climate change. In September, 2016, the UK and China joined forces to scale up cross-border green bond issues to make environmentally friendly projects viable. This action "will play a key role in generating the $100 trillion in green finance needed up until 2030."[8]

Fossil Fuel Industry Leadership

Fossil fuel companies hold great potential for transformation to green energy—and it's in their best interest. If the solar division of French oil company Total SA were separated from its parent company, it would be one of the world's largest solar businesses. Similarly, if Norwegian oil giant Statoil moved its offshore wind business into a separate company, it would be one of the 15 largest companies on the Oslo Stock Exchange.[9]

Shifting a fossil fuel company into renewable energy can be surprisingly simple because many of the needed technical and management skills are the same. Everyone in Statoil's wind energy department was recruited internally, as not much was needed to retrain its engineers. The proceeds from "green bonds" would help the oil companies to shift.

Gubernatorial Leadership

California's Governor Jerry Brown shows the great power governors have to lead their states in addressing climate change. Brown has:

- raised California's mandate for zero-emission vehicles to 15% by 2025
- worked out an eight-state pact on electric cars
- led the creation of a $120 billion green stimulus package, about $20 billion annually through 2020
- created more green jobs than the top four states combined
- mandated that California reduce greenhouse gas emissions to 1990 levels by 2020 and 80% below that level by 2050
- opened the first state-wide cap-and-trade program

in the nation, the second largest carbon trading system in the world

- formed a partnership with Shenzhen, China, to reduce fossil fuels
- formed agreements with Oregon, Washington, Ontario, Quebec, and British Columbia to promote clean-energy jobs and zero-emissions vehicles, and to harmonize energy-efficiency standards and fees for carbon policies
- signed a climate agreement with Mexico – the world's 11th largest carbon emitter – to reduce carbon emissions

Several governors, such as Jay Inslee of the state of Washington, have also exercised strong leadership

Many governors could provide incentives to their K-12 schools to install solar energy systems on school roofs, potentially providing the country with 5.4 gigawatts of solar energy.

Health Professions Leadership

Physicians for Social Responsibility's 50,000 members, including 39 student chapters, work to educate people and to improve national policy formation around nuclear proliferation, global warming, and environmental toxins.

Position statements on climate change have been developed by the American Public Health Association, the American Medical Association, the International Council of Nurses, the Alliance of Nurses for Healthy Environments (who met with senior White House administrators about climate change in 2016), and the Canadian and American Nurses Associations.

Legal Leadership

"When it comes to saving civilization," says Mary Christina Wood of the University of Oregon law school, "law should have a role to play." Wood and others advocate the public trust doctrine (PTD), which holds that all vital resources essential for future civilization are to be held in perpetual trust for all citizens, for all time. This doctrine came down from Roman law and was revitalized in the 1970s and '80s by Professor Joseph Sax, who pioneered U.S. environmental law.

Wood's 2014 book, *Nature's Trust,* characterizes the atmosphere as a trust asset. Atmospheric Trust Litigation (ATL) seeks to impose concrete carbon reduction requirements on governments worldwide, as a fiduciary responsibility taking priority over political objectives. ATL seeks to sue governments, asking the judicial branch to find the executive branch guilty in cases of breach of trust to safeguard the atmosphere. ATL lawyers argue that failure to safeguard the atmosphere amounts to "generational theft," which politicians have ignored because children and future generations do not vote. The courts must step in to protect their property rights.

Individual lawyers and law firms could specialize in suing – or even contribute *pro bono* services to suing – corporations, businesses, and governments who violate climate change agreements, regulations, and principles.

This happened in June, 2015, when a court in The Hague ordered the Dutch Government to cut emissions by 25% by 2020. This class action by the environmental group Urgenda was the world's first climate liability lawsuit – a landmark case that is expected to be copied around the world.[10]

Mayoral Leadership

Mayors are critically important in the climate struggle because urban areas produce about 80% of America's carbon emissions. The COP21 Paris climate summit shined a bright spotlight on international city innovations.

City leaders around the world are joining groups such as the Compact of Mayors, the C40 Cities climate Leadership Group, and the Alliance of Peaking Pioneer Cities, to become greener by learning from each other.

The international organization of megacities, "C40 Cities," has more than 80 members, including New York, London, Toronto, Paris, Moscow, Athens, Berlin, Seoul, Beijing, Singapore, New Delhi, Mexico City, Rio, Buenos Aires, Cairo, and Capetown.

C40 holds regular summits with a focus on climate change collaboration, presenting innovations in financing the green revolution, city-private sector engagement, and mobility management. Collectively they have taken more than 5,000 actions to tackle climate change.

C40's leadership reported in 2014 that city governments alone could cut GHG emissions by 8 billion tons by 2050. The work to stop climate change, said Philadelphia Mayor Michael Nutter, "will be done mostly by mayors. And then we will drive our respective nations' national agendas around these issues."

In America, over 1,000 mayors belong to the U.S. Conference of Mayors, which in 2014 issued a resolution on the need for emergency action:

> The U.S. Conference of Mayors calls on the Administration and Congress to enact an Emergency Climate Protection law that provides a framework and funding for the implementation, in conjunction with state

and local government and the private sector, of a comprehensive national plan to dramatically reduce GHG emissions to avoid catastrophic impacts of climate change on the planet.

Military Leadership

Many military leaders have spoken up on the need to make the U.S. military less dependent on fossil fuels:

- Brig. General Steven Anderson, a former chief of logistics and self-described conservative Republican, said: "Our oil addiction, I believe, is our greatest threat to our national security. Not just foreign oil but oil in general."
- General Gordon Sullivan, former chief of staff of the Army, said: "Climate change is a national security issue. We found that climate instability will lead to instability in geopolitics and impact American military operations around the world."
- Vice Admiral Dennis McGinn (ret.) has said: "The Department of Defense and national intelligence communities recognize [the] clear link between climate change, national security, and instability and have begun strategic plans and programs to both mitigate and adapt to the most likely and serious effects."

Military leaders could state publicly that continued business as usual will make climate adaptation impossible for them to control, and that the military's shift to clean energy will lower emissions substantially and aid national security. Money should be shifted away from the high fuel consumption that is especially harmful to the environment.

They should promote the understanding that, just as the U.S. military played a major role in the WWII battle against fascism through a fully integrated national mobilization, so now a WWII-style climate mobilization backed by the military would help to save civilization.

Peace Activist Leadership

Gore Vidal described the war on terror as "a war both on an unknown enemy, and on an abstract noun – and therefore a war with no end and a war that cannot be won."

This may explain why organized dissent has been lacking against the wars in Afghanistan, Iraq, Libya and Syria (in addition to the fact that the draft has been removed).

The peace movement of the 1960s included activists focused on poverty, civil liberties, nuclear disarmament, and black liberation. These problems are still much in evidence and will worsen with climate change. A resurgence in peace activism focused on climate change would restore common purpose and further the goals of these advocacy sectors by shifting America's focus from wars to domestic needs.

Some have viewed the cataclysmic civil war in Syria as the first climate-change war based on the staggering drought (that turned 60% of the country into desert) and crop failures that preceded it.

Prof. Michael T. Klare, a specialist on war, energy and climate change, believes that the UN climate summits may be viewed as "preemptive peace" conferences. The peace movement (or anti-war movement) could join forces with the climate movement in providing leadership to stave off worldwide instability and the coming climate wars.

Similarly, the network of social movements known as the global justice movement, which opposes corporate globalization and promotes equal distribution of economic resources, is morally positioned to take up emergency climate mobilization as a top priority.

Indeed the time has come for the global climate movement to rename itself "the emergency climate movement," and shape its strategies accordingly.

Religious and Moral Leadership

Those who lead from a moral or religious perspective are essential to mobilizing the country. As James Hansen said, although economic issues are important, the basic issue "is a matter of morality – a matter of intergenerational justice."

In 2015, "The Francis Effect: How Pope Francis Changed the Conversation About Global Warming"[11] described how the views of Americans overall shifted after the release of the Pope's encyclical and visit to the U.S.

Interfaith Power & Light is a large inter-state organization whose mission is to "protect the earth's ecosystem" by being "faithful stewards of Creation by responding to global warming through the promotion of energy conservation, energy efficiency, and renewable energy."

Pastors, priests, rabbis, imams and ethicists could flood newspapers, the Internet, Twitter, and TV/radio programs with the moral case for curbing global warming, so that the country is constantly aware of its need to win this battle, just as Americans were always aware during WWII of the need to defeat fascism.

Republican Leadership

Strong leadership is also needed by concerned Republicans

to turn their party around in Congress, so that it will not continue to thwart the bold changes needed in energy generation.

In December, 2015, *Newsweek* reported a Reuters-Ipsos poll showing that 58% of Republicans said they approved of U.S. efforts to work with other nations to limit global warming.

Scientific American reported a 2016 poll showing a big leap over two years in the number of conservatives who believe in climate change. This was attributed to the lessening of hostility toward the issue by Republican leaders, the visit of Pope Francis, a record-warm winter, and the international Paris agreement of December.

In June, 2016, *The New York Times* reported that Jay Faison, a conservative North Carolina businessman, had committed $5 million through his ClearPath Action fund to back five Republican congressional candidates who support taking climate action.

The call for a carbon tax has also been supported by former senior Republicans such as economist Art Laffer, George Shultz, Reagan's Secretary of State, and former treasury secretary Hank Paulson.

Four former Republican EPA heads told a Senate Committee in 2014 that there is no doubt about the reality and cause of climate change and that the EPA has the authority to regulate greenhouse gases. This EPA authority could go a long way towards implementing a climate mobilization.

Former California governor Arnold Schwarzenegger, Maine Senator Susan Collins, and former presidential candidate Jon Huntsman, wrote a *New York Times* op-ed saying: "Our approach as a party should be one of neither denial nor extremism. Science must guide sensible policy discussions that will lead to well-informed choices, which may mean considering unexpected alternatives."

Scientific Leadership

Scientists feel they are are not permitted to say what is "dangerous" in climate change assessments, or to make recommendations. This is based on an informal prohibition on making "value judgments" and/or making "prescriptive" statements on the issue. Only policy-makers under this understanding can make conclusions on dangers, or make recommendations. This constraint started with the IPCC and is now followed by almost all scientists. It only applies to GHG pollution science.

We therefore need more that anything for government to correct this.

The government or executive needs to make a formal guideline statement that scientists are obliged to draw conclusions and make recommendations on dangers, risks, emergency states, danger and safety limits. The statement would also say that scientists are obliged to make recommendations on best mitigation for safety to governments.

To carry this out, every year the government could request a report from the National Academies specifically on the above. The US Global Change assessments should include these guidelines.

Some scientists are departing from this nonpolitical tradition and going directly to politicians and the public about climate change. In 2016, 31 major scientific organizations in the US – including the American Association for the Advancement of Science, the American Meteorological Society and the Society for Industrial and Applied Mathematics – signed a joint letter to Congress urging them to accept that climate change is real and action needs to be taken.

UK hedge fund manager Jeremy Grantham addressed scientists about taking political action:

> Scientists are understandably protective
> of the dignity of science and are horrified
> by publicity and overstatement. . . . It is
> crucial that scientists take more career
> risks and sound a more realistic, more
> desperate, note on the global-warming
> problem. . . . This is not only the crisis
> of your lives – it is also the crisis of our
> species' existence. I implore you to be
> brave.

"Being brave" would include making strong
public statements and challenging journalists when they
report a false balance between climate science and climate
denial.

NASA's Gavin Schmidt advised fellow scientists:
"It's important for people who know things not to give up
the public sphere to people who don't know things."

In a *New York Times* op-ed, Dr. Michael Mann
explained that whereas at one time he would not speak
publicly about scientific facts, he now feels:

> [T]here is nothing inappropriate at
> all about drawing on our scientific
> knowledge to speak out about the very
> real implications of our research. . . . If
> scientists choose not to engage in the
> public debate, we leave a vacuum that
> will be filled by those whose agenda is
> one of short-term self-interest. There is
> a great cost to society if scientists fail to
> participate in the larger conversation – if
> we do not do all we can to ensure that the
> policy debate is informed by an honest
> assessment of the risks. In fact, it would

be an abrogation of our responsibility to society if we remained quiet in the face of such a grave threat.

Facing the threat, many younger scientists are using the social media (employing methods that will be shown in Chapter 7) to urge mobilization of the country.

Technological Leadership

Many extraordinary technological developments to curb global warming have been described in Dr. Tim Flannery's book, *Atmosphere of Hope: Solutions to the Climate Crisis* (Penguin, 2015). His chapters on new "third way" technologies show us how to draw down many gigatons of CO_2 per year and to naturally and safely store them.

For example, the enormous pressure of the ocean water column would allow CO_2 to be injected into deep marine sediments without escaping. The total storage capacity within 200 miles of the U.S. coastline could hold thousands of years of current U.S. CO_2 emissions.

And the fast-growing edible seaweed farms in North China's Yellow Sea cover 500 square kilometers and yield 400,000 tons of product annually. As it grows, the seaweed takes in CO_2 through photosynthesis, and is removed from the ocean at harvest. This more than reverses local ocean acidification.[12]

And cements that absorb and sequester carbon offer great hope. U.S.-based Solidia Technologies takes CO_2 from industrial waste and incorporates it into a cheaper, stronger, more durable and flexible cement.

And fumes from power plants can be used to make cement, thereby sequestering 90 percent of the CO_2.

Trade Union Leadership

Trade unions have the structure in place to educate and organize their members, and have a long history of leading debate and resistance around social justice issues.

A 2016 study of New Zealand union members showed a strong personal concern for global warming and the unions as important stakeholders and leaders in the action required.

Research head of the British Fire Brigade union, Paul Hampton, wrote in his 2015 book, *Workers and Trade for Climate Solidarity,* "we can't rely on the same businesses and governments who caused the problem to tackle it."[13] He then provides a deep discussion of how organized labor can play a central role in global political efforts to reduce greenhouse gasses.

The International Trade Union Confederation (ITUC) seeks "a just transition" for workers and communities to ensure that all are part of a sustainable, low-carbon economy and benefit from decent green jobs.

In the words of National Nurses United Co-President Deborah Burger, "Nurses in the U.S. and around the world recognize that bold action is needed to challenge the political and economic power of the fossil fuel industry to win health and environmental justice in our communities, to mitigate global warming, and avert a full-scale climate crisis."

Women's Leadership

The Women's Earth & Climate Action Network (WECAN International) has on its board such distinguished figures as Jane Goodall, environmental activist Vandana Shiva, climate scientist Katherine Hayhoe, 350.org director May Boeve, and CNN founder Ted Turner.

WECAN cites Nobel Peace Prize Laureate, Prof. Wangari Maathai, as saying:

> If the international community is serious about addressing climate change, it must recognize women as a fundamental part of the climate solution.

Women everywhere can teach themselves the basics of nonviolent action and social media activism contained in Chapters 6 and 7. Women climate leaders include:

- Franny Armstrong: British documentary film director known for films including *The Age of Stupid*, a reflection from 2055 about climate change
- Gro Harlem Brundtland: Former prime minister of Norway and author of the Bruntland report on Sustainable Development
- Helen Clark: Administrator of the United Nations Development Programme (UNDP), and the 37th Prime Minister of New Zealand (1999-2008)
- Sheila Watt-Cloutier: Canadian Inuit activist who has focused on persistent organic pollutants and global warming
- Christiana Figueres: Costa Rican diplomat who has negotiated climate change instruments since 1995. She became the Executive Secretary of the UN Framework Convention on Climate Change (UNFCCC) in 2010
- Julia Marton-Lefevre: Hungarian environmentalist and Director General of IUCN, the International Union for Conservation of Nature, 2007 to 2014

- Mary Robinson: Barrister, former president of Ireland, UN Commissioner on Human Rights, UN special envoy on climate change, and supporter of fossil fuel divestment
- Marina Silva: Brazilian award-winning environmentalist, Minister of Environment and former colleague of Chico Mendes
- Canadian climate and anti-globalization activist Naomi Klein, author of *This Changes Everything: Capitalism vs the Climate*, and board member for 350.org

A November, 2015 article in *VOGUE Magazine* called "Climate Warriors," interviewed 13 prominent female climate activists. Mindy Lubber, co-founder of Ceres, which mobilizes investor leadership, said:

> I've got a 25 year old son named Abe.
> I've got a 20 year old daughter named Jessie.
> I would throw myself in front of a bus if it was coming at them.
> We all need to throw ourselves in front of this bus called climate change.

Youth Leadership

Young people can play a major role in mobilizing the country through organizations raising awareness that they will be the primary victims of climate disruption:

- *Plant-for-the-Planet,* which plants trees, was inspired by a nine-year-old. Its children met with staff of two Washington state senators, asking that they stop targeting 2°C as a warming limit, because 2°C is catastrophic for kids; that instead they plan to hold warming to 1.2°C and put a price on carbon.

- *Alliance for Climate Education* educates America's high school students about climate change science, providing leadership training on how to take action.

- *C2C Fellows* is "the power network for young people with the wisdom, ambition, talent, and grace to change the future." C2C supports students to envision a path to early, powerful leadership. It stands for "Campus to Congress, to Capitol, to City Hall."

- *Climate Education in an Age of Media* teaches high school and university students to create media pieces on climate change using research, writing, planning, and information technology skills.

- *Gofossilfuel.org* arranges national waves of action to divest colleges and universities from fossil fuels and reinvest in just solutions to the climate crisis.

- *Earth Guardians* is a Colorado-based "tribe of young activists, artists and musicians from across the globe stepping up as leaders and co-creating the future we know is possible." Its 16-year-old climate change activist Xiuhtezcatl Martinez addressed presidential candidates in 2016, demanding #climateactionnow.

- *Energy Action Coalition* involves 50 youth-led environmental and social justice groups focused on winning local elections.

- *Kids vs. Global Warming* was started by Alec Loorz to inform and mobilize kids to take action. Julia Olson, a young environmental lawyer in

Eugene, founded *Our Children's Trust,* helping *Kids* to use the courts to protect the planet. Glori Dei Filippone wrote in 2012:

I am 14 years old. I am sick of global warming. I'm sick of wondering if our world will last much longer...The best way to not worry is to fix the problem... Please contact your Iowa legislators and President Obama on behalf of your kids and grandkids. Ask them to side with the children of this country rather than the fossil-fuel lobbyists.

- *We Are Power Shift* is an online hub empowering the youth climate movement. It is a forum for sharing resources, swapping stories, and strengthening relationships towards youth's vision of a clean, just and sustainable future.
- *Interfaith Youth for Climate Justice* is a Washington, DC-based program for students to spend a year gaining the knowledge, skills and experience needed to become leaders for climate justice.
- *National Wildlife Federation's Campus Ecology Program* engages and educates 1,000 campus communities each year with outreach programs about global warming impacts and solutions.
- *Climate Generation (the Will Steger Legacy)* seeks to empower youth leaders on climate change solutions across the Midwest, through access to decision-makers, funding resources, and training and leadership opportunities.

Once the U.S. president calls for a national mobilization to face the climate change emergency, these

and other organizations could provide thousands of young
people to serve in the cause.

Endnotes

1   "DMOZ is the largest, most comprehensive human-edited
directory of the Web. It is constructed and maintained by a
passionate, global community of volunteers editors. It was
historically known as the Open Directory Project (ODP)."
(https://www.dmoz.org/Society/Issues/Environment/
Climate_Change/Activism/)

2   Ronnie Cummins, "Mother Earth Day 2015: Regenerating
the Soil and Reversing Global Warming," *Organic
Consumers*, April 23, 2015.

3   "The Solution to Climate Change Right Under Our Feet,"
Common Dreams, April 14, 2015.

4   Erica Goode, "Farmers Put Down the Plow for More
Productive Soil," *The New York Times*, March 9, 2015.

5   Max Boykoff, et al, "'Charismatic Megafauna': The
Growing Power of Celebrities and Pop Culture in Climate
Change Campaigns," Department of Geography, King's
College, London, 2010, 2.

6   Risky Business Project, "RISKY BUSINESS: The Economic
Risks of Climate Change in the United States," 2014.

7   The Giving Pledge (http://givingpledge.org/).

8   Emma Rumney, "UK and China join forces to grow
international green bond market," Public Finance
International, September 14, 2016.

9   Alt Energy Stocks Climate Bonds Team, "Fossil Fuel
Companies Should Be Issuing Green Bonds," June, 2016
(http://www.altenergystocks.com/archives/2016/06/fossil_
fuel_companies_should_be_issuing_green_bonds.html).

10   Arthur Neslen, "Dutch government ordered to cut carbon
emissions in landmark ruling," *The Guardian*, June 24, 2015.

11   Edward Maibach, et al, "The Francis Effect," George
Mason University and Yale University. Fairfax, VA:
George Mason University Center for Climate Change
Communication, 2015.

12   Tim Flannery, "Atmosphere of Hope: Solutions to the
Climate Crisis," Penguin, 2015, 52-53.

13   Paul Hampton, "Workers and Trade Unions for Climate
Solidarity," Routledge, Oxford, 2015.

Chapter Six

NONVIOLENT CITIZEN STRATEGIES TO TRANSFORM THE STATUS QUO

Authors' Note: To address possible reservations that ordinary people cannot make a difference, the Appendix offers a Gandhi-style analysis of the citizen as the ultimate source of political power. Readers may choose to read this appendix first.

Opinion polls have shown that the majority of people in approximately 60 countries perceive climate change to be a threat.[1]

In 1998, Dr. Mark Lichbach, professor of government and politics at the University of Maryland, published his "5% rule", which argued that no government can survive an active mobilization of 5% of citizens against its policies.[2]

A more recent study of civil resistance has shown that "no single campaign [against government] has failed after it has achieved the active and sustained participation of just 3.5% of the population."[3] (In the United States, 3.5% is just 11 million people.)

Civil (or civilian) resistance is used in large-scale, organized citizen campaigns to challenge major problems such as unaccountable government, systemic corruption, institutionalized discrimination, environmental degradation, dictatorship, and foreign military occupation. Its methods include nonviolent protests, boycotts, sit-ins, civil disobedience, building of alternative institutions, and dozens of other tactics.

Campaigns become effective because the visibility of civil resistance actions attracts interest and links to security forces, civilian bureaucrats, economic and business elites, educational elites, religious authorities, and the media. As people start to re-evaluate their own allegiances, the size of the movement grows.[4]

When civic mobilization has risen exponentially against government policy, state forces have watched in amazement as the phenomenon of "bandwagon mobilization" unfolded.[5]

Without understanding the latent power of eco-mobilization, many deeply concerned citizens – while doing their best to reduce their own carbon footprints, feel powerless to transform the energy infrastructure that threatens civilization.

These citizens face a systemic threat, made up of three parts:

1. All individuals who by consumption drive the production of fossil fuels
2. The petroleum and automotive industries, which profit most from this production
3. Governments, whose states prosper when their economies, based on energy, are booming

The question is, to which part should their actions be directed?

For an answer, we can turn to the winner of the 1982 Nobel memorial prize in economics, Prof. George Stigler, who explained what we suspect already:

that corporate interests have become intertwined with government policy through "regulatory capture":

> Regulatory capture is the process by which regulatory agencies eventually come to be dominated by the very industries they were charged with regulating. Regulatory capture happens when a regulatory agency, formed to act in the public's interest, eventually acts in ways that benefits the industry it is supposed to be regulating, rather than the public.

Public interest agencies that come to be controlled by the industry they were charged with regulating are known as captured agencies.[6]

With US Government "regulatory capture" now granting fossil fuel subsidies to the tune of more than $37.5 billion per year,[7] climate activists are up against a beast with two heads. Action against each is required.

Citizens, acting together against this two-headed beast, find that they are not powerless. It is encouraging that in May 2016, the Break-Free movement ran a 6-continent "global wave" campaign, involving over 30,000 participants, which disrupted 20 major fossil fuel projects.

It is especially encouraging for climate activists that the regional impacts were covered by the media, including the *Associated Press, Le Monde, Reuters, Spiegel, ABC News, The Nation* (which wrote "Get Ready for a Wave of Green Civil Disobedience, America"), *The Sydney Morning Herald, the Los Angeles Times,* and *The Guardian* (which reported that the "Break Free" fossil fuel protests were deemed the "'largest ever' global disobedience").[8]

Here is an illustrative list of nonviolent actions divided into (1) those aimed at governments, whose regulation is ultimately responsible for energy policy, and (2) those aimed at industry, which is vulnerable to the loss of social acceptance.

I. Actions to Influence Governments

Besides launching a WWII-style mobilization to transition to renewable energy by 2030, the two most important things the US (and other) governments could do to reduce CO_2 emissions would be: (i) impose a nationwide carbon tax; (ii) transfer fossil fuel subsidies to forms of green energy, such as solar and wind.

In calling for any or all of these actions, eco-leaders and citizens have many nonviolent actions from which to choose.

Political Noncooperation

Political noncooperation is the temporary suspension of the usual obedience and cooperation towards a political authority that violates public values. This occurs when people illegally enter a missile base, or when fossil fuel activists enter a coal-fired power plant.

The dominant Western political parties are supported by donations from the petroleum industry, a fact that prompts a conspiracy of silence against the electorate and against life itself. During elections in which global warming is scarcely mentioned, citizens' noncooperation with government may take the form of boycotting government agencies, or legislatures, or symbolic lightning strikes at such locations. People could simultaneously carry big signs in front of the Congress (when in session), the White House, and corporate media offices.

Civil Disobedience

Civil disobedience is a deliberate peaceful violation of particular laws, decrees, ordinances, or military or police commands. It draws its authority from a moral conflict within the individual between the laws of their country and the laws of his or her own conscience. It may be practiced by individuals, small groups, or masses of people.

Far from being frowned upon as a counter-cultural or anti-establishment trend, civil disobedience should be regarded and promoted as being as a sacrifice undertaken by people who have the courage to risk prosecution and disfavor by challenging current social rules.

The government's own employees, officers, and agents may obstruct immoral policies, either openly with explanations or whistle-blowing, or by the quiet blocking and delay of downward orders.

Sympathizers can support civil disobedience by:

- withholding information from police information concerning practitioners
- campaigning actively on their behalf

Judges and juries may dilute the full strength of the law through their interpretation and sentencing, when participating in trials of practitioners.

Police and military personnel may exercise lenience and/or inefficiency in disciplining offenders. There is a large element of personal choice in the degree of severity police officers use in dealing with civil disobedience.

In other parts of the world, the 2015 United Nations awards for energy innovation went mostly to developing countries. These countries, vulnerable to extreme heat, drought, and sea-level rise, could

- halt international conferences, meetings, negotiations, and sports events, including the Olympics, in protest against the failure of highly CO_2 polluting wealthy nations to mobilize decisively
- decline, as a block, to attend United Nations sessions until the wealthy countries introduce a WWII-level conversion to renewable energies.

Nonviolent Intervention Directed Towards Government

Intervention, as its name suggests, is more active and disruptive in its effects than simple noncooperation.

The methods of nonviolent intervention that have been used by human rights causes for decades have been resurfacing internationally for eco-justice.

They include actions in which people are coordinated from a distance to disrupt civil order: At a specific time, banging of pots and pans (as used in front of Iceland's Parliament during the 2008-09 "kitchenware revolution" against the Central Bank[9]), or blowing automobile horns and whistles, or lining the streets or highways at a specific time.

- The *"reverse trial"* is an intervention in which persons supporting an arrested practitioner of civil disobedience in a climate-related court action turn the tables by holding a mock trial, accusing the government of gross negligence in failing to act to address the public threat of climate change as posed by the particular instance at hand. This requires skill and forethought, but can elicit dramatic publicity and support.
- *Sit-ins*: People may use their bodies to physically obstruct business as usual in a place they are not supposed to be. They may enter a government

office or an oil field, and hold a "sit-in" to obstruct normal operations.

- *"Stand-ins"* may take place quietly at the entrances to office buildings, outside meeting halls, or anywhere that officials who have refused to meet public concerns may be sought for interview.
- A variation is the *"mill-in"*, where activists wander around for hours in public buildings and generally disrupt the work. They might wear identical climate-sloganed T-shirts to make their presence visible. It might bear a website URL.
- *Walk-outs*: Practitioners might attend relevant public meetings. As the key speaker begins, one would rise from his seat, call out a climate-related one-sentence statement, then walk out before he can be thrown out. Seated elsewhere, a second can then do the same, then a third, etc.
- *Nonviolent search and seizure*, where people show up with a "citizen's search warrant" seeking information that impacts the public but is hidden from it. For example, the CIA holds classified high-quality global warming data "that could have national security implications," and has been available to only 60 climate scientists.[10]
- *Blockades* are high-profile actions to slow down public services, such as the May 2016 French CGT labor action to block France's oil refineries, fuel depots, and nuclear plants. Similar action could be undertaken in an effort to promote the mass transition to renewable energy and the unemployment problems it would mitigate.
- *Psychological Intervention:* Self-imposed suffering – such as exposing one's self to the elements, damaging one's own property, official

resignations or return or refusal of prestigious awards – puts emotional pressure on other people to re-examine their beliefs about an issue, and often receive surprising publicity and public support.

- *Fasting* (or *the hunger strike*). The endurance of physical suffering or hardship can show deep commitment to a moral issue. Once the initial hunger has passed, the body may feel unexpectedly light and free in a simple, independent way. If thousands of people were to take part in a four or five day fast in a public place, the impact, both on the participants and on the general public, could be very beneficial.

- *"Stall-ins"* reduce ongoing operations to a snail's pace. Any government agency that for example supports fracking or pipelines, can be slowed down by paying taxes to cashiers in coin, or by electronic transfers of ridiculously small amounts to make up the required sum.

- A *"speak-in"* is the respectful interruption of a meeting already in progress in a church, theater, or town hall, to call public attention to a matter of greater urgency. "Guerilla theater" is a politically pointed skit or act presented under the same circumstances.

The success of democracy in the Greek "polis" and in the early American colonies was based largely upon public meetings of the townspeople. Here, popular feeling toward matters of urgency or injustice would build up until a unified action emerged. Experiencing their political problems together, people reinforced one another's concerns and solutions.

Today, however, families watch frightening

weather reports from the isolation of their own living rooms. People *alone* with the news feel small and powerless to effect change in a society where personal power has quietly migrated to government, trans-nationals, and the media. Things are changing somewhat with the empowerment tools offered by Twitter, Facebook, YouTube, blogging platforms, and other social media, to be discussed in the next chapter. But our warming world still cries out for regular, coordinated meetings in towns and communities across the land so that people can feel one another's strength and consolidate national grass-roots action to build a new energy system.

Economic Intervention

Unemployed people have long marched in protest against policies that denied them employment, including marches during the 1890s in Washington, DC, the protests of auto-workers during the Depression, and more recently in Brussels, where European trade unions protested competition from low-wage countries in 2014.

Fossil fuel extraction and infrastructure, which is heavily subsidized by the U.S. and Canadian governments, creates far less employment than would a massive transition to renewable energies and an upgraded electrical grid. Unemployed people could march in protest against these industry-friendly policies that deprive them of meaningful jobs and a safe climate.

National farm policies supporting agribusiness and Monsanto have put many traditional farmers' backs against the wall. In protest against governments that favor dirty energy over future generations, farmers could band together to roll their tractors and farm equipment into towns and city halls, laden with remnants of climate-damaged crops. Local unions could offer support through strikes and slow-downs, together raising awareness of the need to mobilize change.

The greenest transportation modes – rail, electric vehicles, and bike highways – could be buoyed up by consumer demands for subsidies, logistical support, and free advertizing by government and the media.

If other means of action do not work, people can bring pressure with *financial intervention*:

- *Divesting from Government Stocks and Bonds:* Citizens of western governments could bring great pressure to bear on their governments by running broad-based campaigns to withdraw investments in government stocks and bonds – while calling for a full-fledged mobilization to abandon fossil fuels.

- *Withholding the portion of taxes* that pay for fossil fuel subsidies, which in the U.S. are approximately $37.5 billion per year – an average of about $375 per household paying income tax – and putting it in an escrow account for climate preservation projects.[11]

- *Refusing to Pay All Taxes:* As a symbol of protest and a means of withholding all funds from government, ordinary people everywhere could resort to the illegal refusal to pay their taxes. Revenue could be denied from income, property, and sales taxes – and licences for dogs, cars, radios, fishing, and hunting. When large numbers of people resist taxes simultaneously, it overloads the IRS policing capacity.

- *Urging investment banks and financial institutions* to stop financing fossil fuels, and to up the ante on alternatives, making them targets of public action in order to do so. Urging banks and credit unions to gradually reduce credit to individuals and firms involved in fossil fuels.

- *"Total personal non-cooperation,"* a tactic used by conscientious objectors: the refusal to do anything but breathe air, in the face of being jailed, taken to court, required to sign papers, or make promises to improve. Large numbers of people refusing to even walk when arrested, and *going limp* when carried, overwhelms police capacity for discipline.

- *Comply-ins:* A disputed government policy, such as using tax dollars to subsidize fossil fuels, can be met with public over-compliance in other areas, accompanied by a specific demand. Campaigns to overload government departments with excessive compliance – by mailing questions or surplus information in response to address change requirements, surveys, and the census – is a legal method of applying pressure on bureaucracies, which are obliged to file all correspondence.

- Another way to clog the system is to actively *seek imprisonment* through the peaceful breaking of a law or regulation. This is particularly effective if only a few demonstrators have been arrested during a nonviolent action, such as entering a pipeline construction site, when in fact all have broken the law. The rest may press to be jailed also, thereby supporting their companions, overloading costly prison facilities, and gaining publicity for the cause.

- The widespread circulation of flyers and leaflets in a city can provide a blueprint for responsible mass action, explaining the protest issue, and telling where and when to gather peacefully at government locations. During the protest, Twitter and Periscope can be used in tandem (see Chapter 7 on the use of social media) to broadcast the event to the world beyond.

Gven the inexcusable failure of governments to take the lead in preventing the future premature death of billions of innocent people, all forms of non-violent action and civil disobedience seem not only permissible but essential.

II. Actions to Influence the Fossil Fuel and Automotive Industries

In July 2016, five of the top ten Fortune Global 500 companies were oil producers, while two were automakers. Together comprising 70% of the highest revenue companies on earth, they are the best targets for nonviolent action towards industry.[12]

Nonviolent Protest and Persuasion

Formal statements may be directed towards the policies and behaviors of the fossil fuel and automotive industries using:

- Public speeches
- Letters of opposition or support
- Declarations by organizations and institutions
- Signed public statements
- Declarations of indictment and intention
- Group or mass petitions
- Lawsuits for damages

Noncooperation: Economic Boycotting

Consumers, and even suppliers, may decline to purchase goods or services related to the fossil fuel and auto industries in various ways – and if they do so, they should try to make their boycott known, both to the public and the provider:

- *Household goods* that are by-products of fossil fuels are directly vulnerable to economic boycotts from consumers. For example, climate activists should suggest to retail outlets that they stock and promote natural product alternatives to the domestic use of plastics, solvents, detergents, adhesives, and pharmaceuticals. Already, many grocery stores offer alternatives to plastic bags. France has led the way, having banned the use of plastic cups and plates, effective 2020.
- *Retailers* may choose not to handle petroleum-based products. Merchants may hold short "general strikes" to raise awareness of the climate crisis in communities that are dependent upon fossil fuel extraction, while urging conversion to wind and solar energy and storage.
- The massive *home heating oil industry* could be virtually eliminated by replacing residential oil and natural gas furnaces with economical, electrically-driven heat pumps. These act like reverse refrigerators to bring warmth from the outdoor air or ground into the home. Consumers could also demand that heat pumps be phased in through government regulation by 2025.
- *Boycott lists* alerting consumers to companies producing fossil fuel products could be posted online, as well as circulated on the street or outside

retail outlets. By contrast, lists of companies such as Ikea, which uses 100% clean energy, could be compiled and posted alongside, providing alternatives and encouragement to buy only "green."

- *Sponsor speaking tours* for citizens of sinking South Sea Islands in order to support them in urging their governments to place embargoes on the movement of oil tankers into their ports, and to encourage new trade based on solar panels and wind turbines.

Nonviolent Interventions Directed Towards Industry

This list is not exhaustive, but simply illustrative of the kinds of actions that could be taken:

- In a s*it-down strike (or "stay-in")* organized workers, who are usually employed at factories or headquarter offices, take possession of the workplace by "sitting down" at their stations, bringing work to a grinding halt, and preventing their employers from replacing them with strike-breakers. This was seen in the U.S. mass sit-down strike wave of 1933-37 over unemployment. Green technology and jobs await the political will that could be raised by mass strike waves today.
- In *Nonviolent raids,* protesters march to a symbolic site, perhaps a fracking operation, and demand possession of it. Such raids are not meant to actually seize such places, but rather to challenge their policies. This tactic originated with Gandhi's nonviolent raids on colonial salt deposits.
- *Blockades and protest encampments* are

sometimes held at pipeline construction and fracking sites to forestall drilling and ground-water contamination. These may result in publicized police action and copycat rallies across the country.

In June 2016, Al Gore's daughter, Karenna, was arrested with 23 people, including a dozen faith leaders, while protesting construction of a fracked gas pipeline near Boston. Many young people are now blocking fossil-fuel projects, raising publicity, awareness and further action.

In September, 2016, U.S. Green Party leader and presidential candidate, Dr. Jill Stein, and her running mate, Ajamu Baraka, spray-painted in red a bulldozer at a pipeline at the Standing Rock Sioux Reservation in North Dakota. She was charged on an arrest warrant with misdemeanour, trespassing, and mischief.

Amy Goodman, the popular host of *Democracy Now!* and other journalists were punished at the same time for covering the protests against the Dakota Access Pipeline – and reaped the publicity payoff.

- *Lying in the path of a truck or train* can be used to interrupt a delivery. In September, 2016, Scottish protesters stopped a military convoy they believed to be carrying nuclear weapons through Stirling by lying in the road. This could equally be applied to fossil fuel projects.

- *Nonviolent obstruction* goes one step further, when hundreds or thousands of people position themselves to physically obstruct work, vehicles, police or troops, who would have to injure or kill demonstrators to get through.

Workplace Resistance

Once climate protest becomes sufficiently widespread, and public awareness of the need for action has become indisputable, various kinds of strike action may be staged to demonstrate collective feeling towards both industry and government policies. In *protest or token strikes*, workers stop work for five minutes, an hour, a day, or even a week to draw attention to a principle. Labor, which is already organized for its own purposes, is in a unique position to call its vast memberships into protest over the *slow pace* in addressing climate change.

(The unified action by teamsters, steelworkers, mineworkers, shipbuilders, and autoworkers – or by construction, textile, and farm-workers, or by associations of teachers, physicians, nurses, engineers, social workers, biologists, accountants, lawyers, and librarians – could have a tremendous impact.)

- *Slowdowns* in work undermine productivity, reduce profits, clog bureaucracies, and are tricky for management to counter.
- *Working-to-rule* strikes are a variation of the slowdown, in which the employees meticulously follow all the rules and regulations of the union, the employer, and the contract to such technical perfection that productivity is brought to a virtual standstill.
- In *selective strikes* workers decline to do certain jobs. A union discovering that certain materials will be used in fossil fuel extraction may advise workers to abandon these products, pressuring manufacturers to seek contracts outside the oil sector.
- *General strikes* are work stoppages against

major industries at the regional, national, or international level. Strikers could insist that the oil companies and automakers transition to solar energy and electric vehicles – citing the affordable 2017 Tesla Model 3 as the EV and energy storage leading contender.

- An *economic shutdown* is a protest in which labor is joined by management, shopkeepers, restaurateurs, and businessmen to bring economic life in a community to a standstill.

Indeed, once other actions raise climate change to the forefront of public consciousness, it is not unreasonable or unfeasible to think that entire communities might rebel against the suicidal carbon economy, which is poisoning the atmosphere and oceans, and heading planetary life towards extinction.

Endnotes

1   Wikipedia, "Climate change opinion by country" (as of Wikipedia October 2, 2016).

2   Mark Irving Lichbach, "The Rebel's Dilemma," University of Michgan Press, 1998.

3   "The success of nonviolent civil resistance: Erica Chenoweth at TEDxBoulder," Published November 4, 2013 (https://www.youtube.com/watch?v=YJSehRlU34w). This TED talk was based on the article by Maria J. Stephan and Erica Chenoweth, "Why Civil Resistance Works: The Strategic Logic of Nonviolent Conflict," *International Security*, Vol. 33, no. 1, Summer, 2008.

4   Ibid.

5   Ronald A. Francisco, "Dynamics of Conflict," Springer, 2010, p. 55. (http://bit.ly/2b4oZRk).

6   Investopedia, "What is Regulatory Capture?"

7   Oil Change International, "Fossil Fuel Subsidies: Overview," 2016 (priceofoil.org/fossil-fuel-subsidies).

8   Breakfree.org, "May 3–15, 2016: On six continents, thousands of people took bold action to Break Free from Fossil Fuels." For more actions, there is the Swarthmore College *Global Nonviolent Action Database* at http://nvdatabase.swarthmore.edu/ .

9   This action was written up in the Global Nonviolent Action Database (http://nvdatabase.swarthmore.edu/content/icelanders-overthrow-top-power-holders-responsible-economic-crisis-kitchenware-revolution-20).

10   Tim McDonnell, "CIA to close a secretive climate change science program, Grist, May 21, 2015 (http://grist.org/climate-energy/cia-to-close-a-secretive-climate-change-science-program/).

11   Oil Change International, "Fossil Fuel Subsidies: Overview," 2016.

12   The Fortune Global list is at https://en.wikipedia.org/wiki/Fortune_Global_500 Of these 500 companies, 134 are in the US, and 103 in China (as of October 2, 2016).

Chapter Seven

SOCIAL MEDIA STRATEGIES TO TRANSFORM THE STATUS QUO

In the last ten years, the meteoric rise of social media has permeated society.

Social media have transformed citizens from passive receivers of political information into active seekers, interpreters, and producers of news, research, and opinion.

As a result, governments and the media, which dominated political communication for decades, have been forced to relinquish total control over political content and production.

YouTube and other social media have enabled a new generation of political audience to be less dependent on radio and television, to control its own media, and to contribute to the user-generated structure of the Internet.

This growing savvy of the electorate has greatly increased expectations of official transparency. Together with online public opinion leaders, this growing public sophistication has fundamentally altered the political landscape.[1]

Media mogul Rupert Murdoch realized the power of the Internet versus broadcast media when *Fox News* was unable to influence public opinion about the Iraq war.

Powerful alternative information was available online. The same is becoming true of human-caused global warming, which the broadcast media were able to resist for decades.

The Top Social Media Platforms

The extent of social media penetration becomes immediately clear from *Wikipedia's* list of the ten most visited websites in the world, with the top ten including Google, YouTube, Facebook, and Twitter.

Facebook, YouTube, and Twitter are the top three within the social media.[2]

Facebook had 1.65 billion monthly users as of April 2016. Fifty percent of 18-24 year-olds go on Facebook when they wake up, and the average American spends 40 minutes a day on the platform.

YouTube is used by 1.3 billion people, collectively uploading 300 hours of video every minute. Almost 5 billion videos are watched on YouTube every day.

Twitter has 320 million global users and its 140-character micro-blogging platform is widely used for political purposes.

Given these vast networks, citizens can now bring about transformative social changes. With the ubiquity of mobile phones, protest campaigns such as climate marches can now be truly global events.

These social media tools also have enormous potential for raising survival awareness about the need for a climate mobilization.

Twitter

Twitter is now in standard use by politicians, journalists, and citizens as part of a public global network in which political issues and values are considered through mass participation.

Anyone, even without an account, can search Twitter for current political issues. It soon becomes clear that the "twittersphere" (or "twitterverse") is a crucially important social media tool in socio-political activism. Its search engine combined with its vast global interconnectivity can be likened to a collective world brain that includes a focus on global problems.

Here are some ways to build up followers and to spread climate mobilization on Twitter:

- Besides clearly stating your interest and background in environmental and climate issues on your profile, provide a photograph that reflects your central theme.
- Search Google news for up-to-the-minute climate change developments. Then turn to Twitter's search engine to bring up tweets about the Google news items that interest you. Within the stream of tweets rolling by from people all over the world, select the most interesting comments and make contact with their writers.

You can relate to anyone who posts on Twitter using one (or a combination) of four options:

- simply "favorite" the tweet with the star icon
- reply directly to the tweet
- forward the tweet to your own followers with a value-added comment attached
- add the tweeter to the other people that you are following. (If you "follow" a person, you will often be followed back, especially if you have given positive feedback and have an original,

attractive header on your own account.)

- Use "hashtags" to search twitter for people who are interested in your subjects, then reply favorably to their tweets and/or forward them. (Hashtags always begin with the pound sign [#] and act like subject headings in a library catalogue, which uses a controlled vocabulary to take the guesswork out of searching a subject. It's very important to use only hashtags that have been established in the twitter community as currently popular, or that have been used steadily over time.) Lists of strong hashtags, including those related to climate change, are available at two websites that rank them.[3]

- In composing your own tweets, when searching Google News, make sure to sort the returns by date. Tweet these minutes-old news items using one or two highly ranked hashtags. When people search Twitter using these hashtags, your fresh news posts will come up right away and will attract followers.

- Watch the issues on the left sidebar for climate hashtags that are "trending." Tailoring your tweets to trending hashtags will increase your exposure and followers.

- Retweet (RT) celebrity activists such as Mark Ruffalo and Leonardo DiCaprio, who use their large audiences to tweet about dirty energy, pipelines and fracking.

- Use a URL shortener to save space, and note that all URL shorteners include analytics so you can see how effective your links are.

- Embed eye-catching images and videos in your tweets.

- If you have a website or blog, include it in your

Twitter profile. Search Google for your website or blog URL to see how much others are tweeting your page and adjust your tactics accordingly.

- The best times to tweet are between 1pm-3pm from Monday to Thursday, and before 8pm on any day.

Facebook

Although most of Facebook's 1.3 billion users are interacting socially with friends, the platform is also used by virtually all government, corporate, and NGO organizations to profile their activities.

Large climate organizations such as NASA Climate Change and The Climate Reality Project are among thousands of environmental accounts that may be found with the FB search engine.

For the issue of a climate mobilization to become front and center in the lives of everyday Americans and people around the world, Facebook can powerfully connect like-minded people and create a larger awareness of the crisis.

Here are some ways to increase awareness of climate change and to persuade prominent people of the need to act quickly:

- Involve the media. Visit the FB pages of the "big five" US news agencies: CNN, ABC, MSNBC, CBS, and Fox, and check for climate news. Leave constructive comments related to the need for a climate mobilization and include links to other climate news, current YouTube coverage, tweets, books, and articles.
- Search Facebook and Twitter for individual media writers and commentators and post to them directly about the climate emergency.

- Search Facebook's main headings (top and latest stories, people, photos, videos, pages, places, groups, apps and events) for current climate action strategies that you can "like," share with friends or the public, or comment upon.
- On your own page, post images, facts, statistics and hyperlinks to authoritative materials on climate change, and feature people who are taking positive action to address it.
- On Twitter and your FB page, post thought-provoking quotes, such as: "Preventing climate change and adapting to it are not morally equivalent."
- Build a support network around the climate issue; create a web of people to spread the word to their friends and followers.
- Extend the reach of your posts to people beyond your usual circle by including hashtags and tags, and by using the FB video, analytics, and paid advertizing capabilities to expand your campaigns.
- Be original and remember that pithy posts can go *viral* – with thousands or even millions of views, shares, and likes, alerting people to climate change as a personal problem that needs action.

An annual summary, "Global Social Media Research," provides a digital global snapshot of the world's population, internet users, and social media users, including mobile users. It reports that growth in internet users continues at about 10% a year, with mobile users growing at 17%. The over-65s age group is now leading in growth, and the Asia Pacific region leads geographically. (This report reviews other top social platforms such as Instagram, Pinterest, Snapchat, Linkedin, Google Plus, and Tumbler.)[4]

YouTube

With online video production growing at 55% a year,[5] YouTube has become a vital and pervasive political communication tool, which is woven into other social media platforms.

Facebook posts-with-video are shared 12 times more frequently than text-only posts. (Online video has been variously estimated to account for 74% to 80% of all web traffic.) This horizontally-shared material has accelerated the decline in top-down corporate TV viewership.

YouTube has thus become the political pulpit of video choice for climate activists. Accordingly, it is possible for the climate movement to launch compelling educational videos, urge public participation, recruit volunteers, and seek donations.

YouTube offers a level of image-and-message control that is both free and outside the mainstream media. At the same time, it can be shared on Twitter, Facebook, Linkedin, and Snapchat, and it may be retweeted and reposted until a single video can be viewed thousands or millions of times.

Sharing the video platform of their political leaders, climate activists can also post speeches and press conferences to YouTube. They can live-stream their meetings, debates, and conferences on YouTube – which has become the great democratic equalizer in the power of visual communication.

Periscope

Periscope is a live video streaming app for smart phones, owned by Twitter and launched in 2015. Demonstrations, marches, or nonviolent actions can be streamed via

Twitter to the media, twitter lists, or to fellow activists. Periscope was used in a C-SPAN report to broadcast a gun control sit-in from the floor of Congress.

Blogging Platforms

Blogging platforms offer climate activists a simple, time-saving, writing space that does not involve tinkering with websites. They are popular with on-the-go 21-35 year olds, who know they will be severely impacted by climate change. In a 2016 review of the best blogging platforms, the following were included:[6]

- *WordPress.org* powers blogs on more than 60 million websites. Highly customizable and requiring technical skill, it comes pre-installed on most online host providers. A simpler option is the free web-based WordPress.com. WordPress has thousands of theme formats, and is suitable for individual bloggers, publishers, businesses, and complex websites.
- *Google Blogger* (formerly Blogspot) is hosted on Google's free blogspot.com domain. It is simple to learn, does not require coding knowledge, and has a plain interface. It is well suited for first-time individual bloggers, but not for businesses or full-fledged websites.
- *Tumblr* is a free tool that appeals to youth with its mobile app, and is quick and easy to learn. A mix between a full-fledged blog and Twitter, Tumblr is designed for frequent posts of short messages and images, but is not suitable for long-article blogging.
- *Medium* is a free, easy-to-learn social journalism platform that allows images but does not offer

much customization. It has a simple Word-like page format and requires no coding knowledge. Connected to Twitter, Medium enables wide viewing of content on a clean, minimal platform, and is suited to freelance writers and authors.

Posting Reader Comments to Online News Stories

Commenting on news stories is an art that can become surprisingly influential, although in 2014 some news outlets started closing down their comments sections.

Papers such as the *Huffington Post* and *The Guardian* encourage registered reader comments, and here people can build up substantial followings.

The New York Times, which receives about 9,000 comments a day, wrote that reader voices "have enhanced our journalism, offering new information, insight and analysis on many of the day's most pressing issues."

NYT's top commenter, Gemli, writes about fact-based policy, climate change, and equality. He averages 354 reader recommendations per comment, and said, "The first sentence of the comment is key, and it's usually the hardest to write. I can spend a half-hour writing and rewriting the first line... Reading conservative pundits usually gets my goat, especially when they're denying climate change."[7]

Wikis

Teams of people working together for climate mobilization might consider a wiki platform, which is a website that allows collaborative editing of content and structure by its users.

From within their browsers, people may add

content through easy visual editing, with no training required.

Wikis are used extensively in education, so students are familiar with how the platform works. Wiki features include publishing content, sharing documents, and team collaboration, making it useful for cooperative climate change work.

By default, a wiki is private to a group, but it may be made public for open collaboration, like *Wikipedia*.

There are a number of wiki engines available. Three wiki services that are free for education, and economical for other purposes, are wikispaces.com, wikidot.com, and pbworks.com.

Also, wikiHow.com offers open, editable content on how to do almost anything, including how to use social media to become an activist.[8]

Online Petition Sites

Online petition websites allow people to discover, support and organize campaigns, fundraisers, and petitions around issues that impact the community and the world.

However, there is a learning curve involved. To be effective, it's important to know the ropes of writing and submitting a petition before making an attempt.[9]

Trending petitions may be seen at change.org, causes.org, and avaaz.org.

Podcasting

Today is said to be the golden age of podcasting, and indeed climate change podcasts may be easily found by googling.

For example, a Tom Steyer and Andy Karsner podcast on following up on the 2015 Paris climate summit was posted June 2, 2016.[10]

Podcasting is a very effective way to broadcast ideas, usually in a series, into the audio world. It is much easier to produce a regular podcast show than a video series or other forms of online content, but it requires some initial time and equipment to get set up, as explained in a July, 2015 article.[11]

Conclusion

The "participatory web," also known as the Web 2.0, has established itself as the second stage of development of the Internet, which has moved from static web pages to dynamic, user-generated content and the growth of social media.

Millions of users are learning to create and share content through not only the social media, but also through wikis, blogs, and podcasts.

The social media are therefore major forums, in which the battle to implement a full climate mobilization – the only timely response remaining to head off global warming – will be played out around the world.

Endnotes

1   LaChrystal D. Ricke, *The Impact of YouTube on U.S. Politics* (Barnes & Noble, 2014).

2   David Chaffey, "Global Social Media Research Summary, 2016," August 8, 2016 (http://www.smartinsights.com/social-media-marketing/social-media-strategy/new-global-social-media-research/).

3   The website https://ritetag.com allows you to enter a strong hashtag, such as #keepitintheground, and then it will produce a list of associated strong ones, and their number of tweets and retweets per hour (https://ritetag.com/best-hashtags-for/keepitintheground).
      A second website (http://gethashtags.com/twitter/tag/Keep-

ItintheGround) lists the top 50 Twitter hashtags associated with the one you like. Here is a list of established climate hashtags related to #KeepItintheGround: #actonclimate, #ClimateChange, #COP21, #oil, #coal, #climate, #SaveTheArctic, #Solar, #fossilfuels, #EndCoal, #fracking, #FossilFuel, #pollution, #Carbon, #Arctic, #renewableenergy, #climateaction, #saveoursolar, #guardian, #divestment, #renewables, #tarsands, #endofcoal, #energy, #fossilfree, #GHG.

4   Chaffey, "Global Social Media Research Summary, 2016."
5   Ricke, *The Impact of YouTube on U.S. Politics.*
6   "Top 5 Best Blogging Platforms," *Beebom*, June 2, 2016.
7   Bassey Etim, "Meet Some of Our Top Commenters," *New York Times*, November 23, 2015.
8   "How to Become a 21st Century Social Activist" (http://www.wikihow.com/Become-a-21st-Century-Social-Activist).
9   Guidelines for writing and submitting petitions are available on the main petition websites, at Citizens for Public Justice (in Canada), and at http://www.thepetitionsite.com/successful-petition-format/.
10   "Tom Steyer & Andy Karsner, "Making Good on the Promise of Paris," climateone.org, June 2, 2016.
11   Hesse, "How to make a successful podcast."

Chapter Eight

MOVING TOWARD
A NEW MINDSET

This juncture in time may be the most important in human history.

The situation has been left so long – has become so critical – that our collective action or inaction during the next five years will likely decide whether we even have a future.

In June, 2015, Pope Francis referred to the narrow, outdated mindset that has enabled profound neglect:

> It is remarkable how weak international political responses have been.... There are too many special interests, and economic interests easily end up trumping the common good and manipulating information so that their own plans will not be affected.... Consequently the most one can expect is superficial rhetoric, sporadic acts of philanthropy and perfunctory expressions of concern for the environment, whereas any genuine attempt by groups within society to introduce change is viewed as a nuisance

based on romantic illusions or an obstacle
to be circumvented.[1]

Citizens must urge their governments to wake up and embrace the full reality of climate disruption – then take *dramatic action.*

A specific first move could be for national leaders worldwide to adopt the life-saving approach used by President Franklin Delano Roosevelt to solve a crippling problem during the Great Depression.

In 1935, the United States was in a deep social and economic crisis. The wind-swept prairies were a dust bowl of drought. Unemployment was high, and the country was hungry.

Worse yet, the prohibitive costs of power-line construction meant only 10% of isolated rural farming communities could afford electricity from private electric companies. Farmers left for work in the cities and the Depression deepened.

To address the crisis, Roosevelt created, by Executive Order, the Rural Electrification Administration (REA). He allocated funds for rural electrification, granting low-interest loans (applied for through state authorities) to municipalities, people's electricity districts, and cooperatives. The REA provided field visits to farms, offered technical support from specialists, and mailed out bulletins and memoranda.

This action led to almost 1,000 energy cooperatives, some of which still operate today. By 1955, 97% of farmers had electricity. Following World War II, this state-cooperative partnership was successfully copied elsewhere, including the Philippines, Costa Rica, and China.

The massive transition to renewable energy we need today is not qualitatively different from the U.S. rural energy deficit in 1935. We need the same high levels of planning and coordination to ensure the right mix of solar, wind, hydro, geothermal, wave, and tidal energies in a framework that will guarantee democratic control over local energy production across the country.

The US President could at any time issue an Executive Order to create a "Renewable Energy Administration", with the authority and funding to spring into action immediately. (The President could urge the United Nations Environmental Program and the UN Framework on Climate Change to recommend the model to other countries.)

Pressing problems, such as drought, wildfire, flooding, excessive heat, water shortage, and crop destruction could be addressed through presidential actions based on the social and economic policies of Roosevelt's New Deal program.

An Emerging Mindset for Civil Society

The general public, although favorable to clean energy, has not yet been overwhelmed by climate change as an urgent personal problem.

However, 2015 and 2016 showed that we might yet rise to our existential crisis.

NASA reported July 2016 as the hottest month in history. With heat records being shattered month by month, the stark reality of climate change is finally dawning. The same is true in relation to excessive rain and flooding.

However, the obstacles to a mass awakening persist.

Plato once wrote:

"You cannot be both powerful in the state
and unlike it in character....

You must be no mere imitator, but essentially like them, if you mean to achieve any genuine sort of friendship with Demus the Athenian people."[2]

The character of the state is nowhere more evident than at the annual World Economic Forum held in Davos, Switzerland, attended by privileged elites with a neo-liberal agenda of free trade, deregulation, and public-private cooperation.

Although this economic forum pays lip service to climate change, it is funded by the 100 top corporations in the world. These corporations set the agendas and invite heads of government as their guests to discuss them.

The impact of these agendas on trade agreements, globalization, unemployment, poverty, and climate degradation is pervasive, drawing protests and blockades from environmentalists and trade unions.

The World *Social* Forum (WSF), on the other hand, was conceived in Brazil in 2001 as an alternative to the World Economic Forum. Here, civil society organizations, trade unions, and NGO's seek to design an alternative future informed by the "bottom-up" visions and values of local initiatives.

The World Social Forum represents *the character of earth's citizens*. In its own words, it is "committed to building a planetary society directed towards fruitful relationships among Mankind and between it and the Earth."[3]

Pope Francis said:

The gravest effects of all attacks on the environment are suffered by the poorest.

He also condemned the sense of privilege at the problem's core:

In practice, we continue to tolerate that some consider themselves more human than others, as if they had been born with greater rights.

This kind of privilege is precisely what the World Social Forum is trying to change.

The central theme of its enormous 2016 meeting in Montreal,[4] attended by 35,000 people, was to build a convergence of actions that will lead to social and ecological justice for the emergence of "another world".

This mindset rejects both privilege and poverty on a global scale.

World poverty has been recently linked to the new idea of "extractivism".

Extractivism is exploitation by northern countries of the minerals and fossil fuels in southern countries, whereby southern wealth migrates north. The resulting unemployment and poverty in the south have gone hand in hand with the CO_2 emissions spewed by northern wealth.

Extracting fossil fuels is obsolete. The World Social Forum has set itself the task of moving to a global "post-extractive" economy.

The WSF mindset needs to take hold at all levels of society. Once underway, there will be many roads towards exciting and dynamic change.

One such road is a superb two-hour presentation by 25-year climate activist and eco-futurist Guy Dauncey – who has assembled in his 2016 video, "Journey to the Future,"[5] an amazing array of international CO_2-beating actions and technologies that have seldom been reported elsewhere.

This film shows the surprisingly pervasive engagement of civil society with "emergency climate mode". Although it has been downplayed by the corporate media, this engagement is becoming our new paradigm, and it is beginning to feel unstoppable.

We saw that in 2016, the Democratic National Convention approved a WWII-style emergency climate mobilization – but predictably it did not make the mainstream news.

However, on August 15, 2016, the *New Republic* published a landmark article by 350.org founder Bill McKibben, who declared in no uncertain terms that our only hope for survival is a WWII-style climate mobilization. In a refreshing change, this article was widely picked up by the corporate media.

We end this book by offering incentive to those who have not yet begun their journey with the climate mobilization movement. In the words of Russell Greene:

> It's too much to hold. And so we blink
> – and move on – back to gradualism.
> Clinging to the false hope that somehow
> what it is that we always have done will
> work this time. It's our own type of
> denial. No – certainly not denial like
> the Republican climate deniers – but,
> nonetheless, a dangerous denial.
> We must step inside. We can and must rise
> to this moment. Imagine your children's
> lives. Step inside that. Become your
> child – not today – but in 30 or 40 years.
> And, as your child – ask yourself—
> "Mom? Dad? What happened? Why
> didn't you do something?"
> Can you step into that? And, can you
> stay there? Because if you do – if we do,
> if we step into that truth, and stay there –
> we'll know what to do.[6]

Endnotes

1   "Encyclical Letter, Laudato Si' of the Holy Father Francis, On Care For Our Common Home," No. 54, May, 2015 (http://w2.vatican.va/content/francesco/en/encyclicals/documents/papa-francesco_20150524_enciclica-laudato-si.html).

2   Plato, *Gorgias* 513b, trans. W.R.M. Lamb, *Plato in Twelve Volumes*, (Cambridge: Harvard University Press, 1967), Vol. 3.

3   The World Social Forum defines itself as "an opened space – plural, diverse, non-governmental and non-partisan – that stimulates the decentralized debate, reflection, proposals building, experiences exchange and alliances among movements and organizations engaged in concrete actions towards a more solidarity, democratic and fair world" (http://www.thesynergycentre.org/brighton-social-forum/).

4   This Montreal World Social Forum was attended by 35,000 people – about the size of the 2015 Paris climate summit, COP21 – the largest meeting in France since 1948. Although the WSF was running 170 events simultaneously in Montreal universities, the Forum received mostly marginal and dismissive mainstream media coverage. It was a disgrace that people who wanted to participate from around the world, particularly from Africa, were denied visas by Canadian embassies. These things demonstrate Plato's point about state resistance to the values of civil society.

5   Guy Dauncey, "Journey to the Future" (https://www.youtube.com/watch?v=iJHuam61Vrc). Guy Dauncey is an eco-futurist who works to develop a positive vision of a sustainable future, and to translate that vision into action.

6   Russell Greene, "Beyond Paris: Finding the Courage to Face the Climate Emergency," Common Dreams, July 19, 2016 (http://www.commondreams.org/views/2016/07/19/beyond-paris-finding-courage-face-climate-emergency).

AFTERWORD

Chicago, Summer 2048

Looking back, it was amazing. Today, we take it for granted that our city operates entirely on renewable energy, and that all farms are organic. We think it normal that every rooftop is solar, and every car, bus and truck is electric. And we are very comfortable with our new restored democracy.

It's not as if the climate crisis has lessened. The appalling heat waves, last summer's dramatic flood, the steady sea-level rise—they're all still happening, not just here but all over the world, and they will continue for many years to come. But the outlook for the future has changed, thanks to the worldwide climate mobilization, which led to the Great Transition that took place in the 2020s.

By 2016, the rise in global temperature had become so alarming that the U.S. Democratic National Committee and the U.S. Green Party both adopted the need for a WWII-style climate mobilization. The idea caught on in the social media, rapidly spreading across the United States and to other countries.

The pressure from the climate marches and the newly formed Climate Action Circles became such that the media could no longer ignore them. Labor unions and professional associations supported the call, and delegations of children with their grandparents visited their federal representatives, urging action. Senators and members of Congress surprised everyone by making impassioned public appeals to the President to wield emergency presidential powers: to declare a climate emergency and order a rapid transition from fossil fuels to renewable energy.

The growing groundswell of public support, coupled with evidence about how a new green economy would bring jobs and growth and growing confidence in 'the new American Dream' gave the President and Congress the political space needed to order a full-scale energy transition. Fossil fuel companies were ordered to reduce their production and energy imports by 10% a year, while utilities and the auto industry were ordered to increase the production of renewable energy and electric vehicles by the same amount. The new Federal Bank for Public Renewal provided back-up finance, and affected regions were provided with community economic development and extended personal re-employment support to counter the job-losses.

Throughout the decade, people kept organizing, one teach-in, rally or gathering after another, until they got the right people elected, the Citizens United Supreme Court ruling overturned, and campaign finance limited to a single $1,000 political donation a year. The vision of a new cooperative economy steadily became a reality.

Today, even though the climate crisis will continue throughout the lives of my grandchildren, there is a realistic prospect that global emissions will fall to zero within the decade, and that over time, the changes in the way farmers, ranchers and foresters are managing the land will enable nature to re-absorb the carbon surplus that has built up in the atmosphere. It will be a rough ride, but not a hopeless one.

—**Guy Dauncey**
author of *Journey to the Future: A Better World is Possible*. See www.earthfuture.com and www.journeytothefuture.ca.

THE CITIZEN AS THE ULTIMATE SOURCE OF POLITICAL POWER

Although this book has proposed workable strategic actions for the visible leadership of government and the media, it is ultimately the people whose will, power, and cooperation are most essential in the drive for planetary survival.

As extreme weather events escalate in severity and regularity, awareness of the need for urgent transformation to clean energy is sweeping the planet.

But our outdated energy system cannot be transformed in time to save civilization unless an active and relentless force emerges to disrupt it. A "massive interventionist democracy" could tip the scales towards a full WWII-style mobilization against runaway global warming.

A majority of our citizens would like to see this, but believe that the energy system is so entrenched that only violent revolution could stop it – yet they reject violence.

They are also in the habit of obeying power, which for the most part they believe to be legitimate. Many feel unqualified to protest it. Some fear sanctions against resistance. Others lack self-confidence, avoiding responsibility and delegating their responsibility upwards. In sum, many people feel impotent to resist the power above them.

But this is a misunderstanding – a mistaken assumption about the nature of political power.

In fact there are two ways of viewing political power.

The first view is that ordinary people are subordinate to the government and dependent upon its decisions, good will, and support.

The second view is that government power is conditional upon the decisions, goodwill and support of the people.

The first theory of power ignores the fact that the source of a government's power depends intimately on the obedience, cooperation, and assistance of the population. All rulers require the skills, knowledge, labor, advice and administrative ability of much of the population they govern.

But the second theory – that government power *is* the power of the people – suggests that at any time the people may withdraw or reclaim the power that has been theirs from the start.

The crucial thing about these opposing assumptions is that either one can become self-fulfilling if enough people believe in it and act upon it.

The crux of the matter is that power is not intrinsic to rulers: the political power that rulers have comes from the society which they govern. Political outcomes are largely determined by whether or not people perceive themselves as the ultimate source of political power.

Opinion polls conducted in 2016[1] show that today's governments are playing close to the limits of citizen tolerance for climate catastrophe – an issue that has driven huge climate marches in 2014 and 2015 but has not yet been universally protested.

But civic obedience has persisted because, although government is actually only a ruling minority, its hierarchical organization allows its parts to act in concert, and its citizens to be dealt with one by one.

The solution, then, lies in transforming the silent general opposition to fossil fuels into a united public outcry for a WWII-type government mobilization that will rapidly lead an emergency conversion to 100% clean energy.

This means that everybody, everywhere, who is opposed to fossil fuels could view himself or herself as part of a single political force that earnestly seeks leadership and unification.

What is urgently needed is a unified *vision* of a "massive interventionist democracy," through which a world-wide network of climate activists – such as youth groups, women's groups, trade unions, professional groups, churches, anti-war groups, and global justice groups[2] – would focus unrelenting pressure upon their governments to mobilize action against the climate emergency.

The coordinating headquarters of this new emergency climate movement would need to educate its members in the many techniques of nonviolent action, a selection of which are included in Chapter 6.

The primary candidate for the job might be Bill McKibben, founder of 350.org, who since 2009 has been coordinating global climate campaigns, including the September, 2014 New York City People's Climate March of more than 300,000 people, with companion demonstrations running globally.

Another candidate, which is already promoting massive activism, is Al Gore's *Climate Reality Project,* with nearly 50 staff and 7 branches. Under Gore's dynamic leadership, it could be greatly expanded.

A further visionary initiative is Canada's "Leap Manifesto," which seeks 100% renewable energy for Canada by 2035, with the first slate of green jobs going to those who need employment most – thus binding climate solutions to the reduction of poverty as also envisioned in the Pope Francis *Encyclical* of June, 2015.

But it's vital to keep in mind that people will not commit themselves to political goals without some expectation of success. It cannot be repeated too often that when we withdraw our obedience and cooperation in sufficient numbers for long enough, governments must inevitably bow to our will.

As citizens of Western countries, we have the power to bring our governments under control. We only need to understand this fact and act upon it.

Endnotes

1   Lydia Saad and Jeffrey M. Jones, "U.S. Concern About Global Warming at Eight-Year High," Gallup, March 16, 2016. This poll showed that 64% of US adults are worried "a great deal or a fair amount" about climate change. Richard Wike, "What the world thinks about climate change in 7 charts," Pew Research Center, April 18, 2016. "Majorities in all 40 nations polled say climate change is a serious problem, and a global median of 54% believe it is a very serious problem… Two-thirds believe people will have to make major lifestyle changes to combat climate change."

2   Pope Francis linked the global justice movement to the climate change movement in his June, 2015 *Encyclical.*

RECOMMENDED READING

Lester Brown, *Plan B 4.0: Mobilizing to Save Civilization*, W.W. & Norton Company, 2009.

Lester Brown, *The World on Edge: How to Prevent Environmental and Economic Collapse*, Norton, 2011,

Tim Flannery, *Atmosphere of Hope*, Penguin, 2015.

Russell Greene, "Beyond Paris: Finding the Courage to Face the Climate Emergency," *Common Dreams*, July 19, 2016.

David Ray Griffin, *Unprecedented: Can Civilization Survive the CO2 Crisis?* Clarity Press, 2015.

James Hansen et al., "Target Atmospheric CO_2: Where Should Humanity Aim?" *Open Atmospheric Science Journal* 2 (2008), 217-31.

Bill McKibben, "We're under attack from climate change—and our only hope is to mobilize like we did in WWII." *New Republic*, August 15, 2016 (https://newrepublic.com/article/135684/declare-war-climate-change-mobilize-wwii).

Oil Change International, "Fossil Fuel Subsidies: Overview," 2016.

Joseph Romm, *Climate Change: What Everyone Needs to Know*, Oxford University Press, December, 2015.

Margaret Klein Salamon, "Leading the Public into Emergency Mode: A New Strategy for the Climate Movement," 2016.

Margaret Klein Salamon, "The Case for Climate Mobilization," 2015.

"Bernie Sanders: We Must Move on Climate as We Would if We Were at War," Climate Emergency Declaration, 13 May 2016. For video, see "Bernie Sanders Talks Climate – and WWII-Scale Mobilization" (https://www.youtube.com/watch?v=4hSwVUZC5Eo).

Ezra Silk, "The Climate Mobilization Victory Plan," The Climate Mobilization, August, 2016. (Foreword by Paul Gilding).

Philip Sutton, *Striking Targets: Matching Climate Goals with Climate Reality,* Breakthrough National Center for Climate Restoration, Melbourne, 2015.

Swarthmore College, Peace and Conflict Studies, *Global Nonviolent Action Database.*

YEARS of Living Dangerously (http://yearsoflivingdangerously.com/).

INDEX